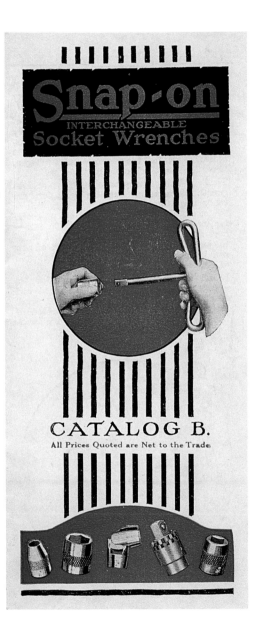

Snap-on
INTERCHANGEABLE
Socket Wrenches

CATALOG B.

All Prices Quoted are Net to the Trade

AMERICA'S 100 YEAR LOVE AFFAIR WITH THE AUTOMOBILE

AND THE SNAP-ON TOOLS THAT KEEP THEM RUNNING

David K. Wright

Motorbooks International
Publishers & Wholesalers ®

First published in 1995 by Motorbooks International Publishers & Wholesalers, PO Box 2, 729 Prospect Avenue, Osceola, WI 54020 USA

Motorbooks International books are also available at discounts in bulk quantity for industrial or sales-promotional use. For details write to Special Sales Manager at the Publisher's address

Library of Congress Cataloging-in-Publication Data

Wright, David K.
     America's 100 year love affair with the automobile/David K. Wright.
         p. cm.
     Includes index.
         ISBN 0-7603-0036-4
     1. Automobiles--United States--History. 2. Automobiles--United States--Maintenance and repair--Equipment and supplies--History. 3. Snap-on (Firm)--History. I. Title.
TL23.W75   1995
629.23--dc20   95-22538

On the frontispiece: Early Snap-on catalog cover.

On the title page: A 1920s-era Snap-on dealer visits a mechanic in this re-enactment.

On the back cover: Top: Spotless 1930s General Motors dealership in Ohio. Bottom: Snap-on is very involved in motorsports sponsorship. Here, Al Unser, Jr., leads Paul Tracy through the streets of Long Beach in 1994. *George Tiedemann*

Printed in Hong Kong

TABLE OF CONTENTS

PREFACE

A writer several years ago labeled Snap-on Tools "a conservative innovator." Accurate as that label may be, it just doesn't do this billion-dollar-a-year company justice.

In several very real ways, the history of Snap-on *is* the history of the automobile in this country. True enough, cars were here to stay by the time Joseph Johnson decided in 1920 that five thoughtfully designed and carefully constructed tools could do the work of fifty. But Snap-on grew rapidly once it got started, catching up to automobile manufacturing in several ways.

Besides making mechanics more productive—and being incredibly attentive to their wants and needs—over the years Snap-on provided automakers themselves with the hand tools and equipment necessary to become increasingly innovative.

Tools for the assembly line, tools for the dealership, tools for the independent shop, tools for the race track—Snap-on has anticipated automotive needs like few other companies.

In the process, it has become the company that other tool companies look to for innovation. And they have earned money, had fun, and made hundreds of thousands of jobs better and easier.

Snap-on Incorporated can't wait for its seventy-sixth year and America's second automotive century to begin.

Snap-on's first production facility was on Reed Street in Milwaukee, Wisconsin.

6

INTRODUCTION

*T*here were cars, or approximations of cars, in the United States beginning in the 1890s. There were hand tools, or their approximations, too. And while it took more than thirty years for automobiles to reach a threshold of real reliability, the first quality extension of man's ability in the way of tools took place in 1920—the year Joseph Johnson conceived the Snap-on idea. Both automobiles and hand tools have roots deep in America's Industrial Revolution.

The Industrial Revolution began in the United States during the presidency of James Monroe, around 1820. Breakthroughs such as Eli Whitney's cotton gin and Seth Thomas's clock hinted at even grander things to come. Steam engines soon provided power and, once track was laid, the country was conquered inevitably during a period when inventions became almost routine news.

Eventually, Americans paused to realize they had devoured the vast frontier that had always spread before them. Their restless energy turned to making life easier and more productive as the United States continued to take the Industrial Revolution very seriously. New World ingenuity showed in everything from the linotype printer (1884) to the Kodak still camera (1888) to a machine that automatically filled bottles (1895). Citizens opened their penny newspapers to find reports of inventions such as the fountain pen (1884), the phonograph record (1887), and the zipper (1891).

Foreign inventions and discoveries filled the daily news as well: steam turbines (1884, England), radio signals (1894, Italy), and tape recorders (1899, Denmark), as well as breakthroughs such as the mysterious x-ray (1895, Germany), and a potent bodily substance called adrenalin that oozed from a gland near the kidneys (1901, Japan). But nothing would have the worldwide effect of a German contraption, unveiled in 1889 by a man named Gottlieb Daimler. This was, of course, the first functioning, gasoline-powered, internal-combustion, four-wheel automobile.

No other contrivance has had so much impact on the United States.

As early as 1906, Cadillacs such as this model were setting quality standards. The vehicles had more interchangeable parts sooner than virtually any other make and were known for the quality of materials. *Used with permission, General Motors Media Archives*

1906 MODEL
CADILLAC.

One

THE EARLY YEARS, 1891-1920

1996 marks the automobile's centennial in the United States, and the contention that the first real American automobile was Henry Ford's 1896 Quadricycle is a strong one. It had four wheels, it was reliable, and it was built in Detroit. Ford's accomplishments soon overshadowed his predecessors. As early as 1891, for example, F.W. Lambert was chugging noisily around Ohio City, Ohio, aboard a handmade, self-propelled, single-cylinder, internal-combustion, three-wheeled vehicle fueled with gasoline. (Significantly, some fifty miles to the southeast, the progressive city of Bellefontaine, Ohio, poured the world's first concrete street that same year.) Two Spring-

That's Louis Chevrolet at the wheel of the first Chevrolet prototype, completed in March 1911. Chevrolet was a racer and a creator of speed parts for Fords and other makes. Chevrolet was a familiar name to Midwest racing fans throughout the teens. *Used with permission, General Motors Media Archives*

The original set of Snap-on tools, as constructed by Joe Johnson and Bill Seidemann.

field, Massachusetts, bicycle mechanics named Duryea constructed their four-horsepower, single-cylinder Motor Wagon in 1893, and within months there were hordes of midnight machinists and after-hours fabricators working on their own versions of powered vehicles. The Duryeas in 1895 were the first Americans to produce salable cars.

Other pioneering efforts included Elwood Haynes, the Kokomo, Indiana, natural-gas company superintendent; Ransom Olds, who worked for his father in a Lansing, Michigan, machine shop; and George B. Selden, an attorney and inventor from Rochester, New York. Selden filed patent No. 549,160, on May 8, 1879, for the creation of the automobile. The patent was granted on Nov. 5, 1895, and contained his claim to the "original application of the internal-combustion hydrocarbon motor to a road vehicle," though Selden failed to ever produce in quantity.

Who put together America's first internal-combustion engine? There are as many answers as designs, but among the first was a father-son team from Sterling, Illinois, by the name of John and James Charter. The Charters received a patent for a gasoline engine on Jan. 9, 1893, displaying the single-cylinder device at the Columbia Exposition, a world's fair held in Chicago. (Also the site and date of the first foreign car exhibited in the U.S., a German Mercedes.) The engine featured a scary and haphazard method of squirting raw fuel into an intake pipe, since a carburetor was a rare commodity in those days. And because the Charters considered electricity dangerous, early models used something called a hot-tube ignition—a small platinum piece screwed into the cylinder head. Nevertheless, tinkerers and manufacturers alike bought Charter and other ready-made engines for the vehicles of their dreams.

Father John Charter held at least eleven patents, granted between 1893 and 1896. The inventor constructed several engines himself, turning to H.W. Caldwell & Son in Chicago when demand exceeded supply. The Windy City firm was experienced at assembly, having put together a six-cylinder, sixty-five-horsepower engine that was the largest gasoline-powered design of the time. Charter's modest, single-cylinder thumper would be among the very first commercially successful, mass-produced, internal-combustion engines. It would power generators, pumps, railway cars, farm equipment, and of course, automobiles.

America's heroes at the time quickly gravitated to automobiles. A car by itself was big news on most streets, but if it had a celebrity passenger, the mere presence made headlines. William F. Cody (Buffalo Bill), with his flowing mane and pointed beard, was seen in so many photos with cars that it became obvious he favored automobiles over horses. William McKinley became the first president to ride in an automobile, and Mark Twain was a regular passenger in cars belonging to various friends and admirers. Other luminaries in cars included Teddy Roosevelt, baseball stars Honus Wagner and Ty Cobb, and temperance agitator Carry Nation. Nicholas II, Russia's last czar, owned a fleet of American White cars and trucks.

No sooner did folks get their hands on cars, than they began to misbehave. The first auto accident took place in New York City in 1896 when Henry Wells, at the tiller of a Duryea, struck Evelyn Thomas, a bicycle rider, fracturing her leg. Wells spent the night in jail. The first fatality was recorded that same year in New York City. Henry H. Bliss, a sixty-eight-year-old real-estate broker, was run over as he stepped off a street car near Central Park. Driver Arthur Smith was arrested and held on $1,000 bail. And speaking of arrest, America's first speeding violation took place in 1899 a few blocks away on Lexington Avenue. Jacob German was pinched in his electric cab for driving at the "breakneck speed" of twelve miles per hour.

Cars moved ahead—or failed to do so—thanks to some of the most godawful means of power ever conceived. Steam engines perked along, as did natural gas and diesel machines. But the fuel of choice was gasoline, a distillate of crude oil. Crude seeped plentifully from the ground from Pennsylvania to California, so there was inexpensive fuel for the dozens of internal-combustion gasoline engines by the time the twentieth century dawned. As a matter of fact, the first significant oil find in Texas took place near Beaumont in 1901. Combusting petroleum and air and transmitting that power, often via slapping leather belts or by clattering chains, was a great source of excitement.

Internal combustion competed with electricity and steam early in the twentieth century. Among the more bizarre steam advocates were the Stanley brothers, bearded, middle-aged twins who dressed alike and thereby helped grab publicity for their

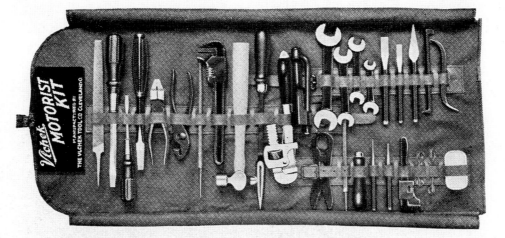

Motorist Kit

No. 902

Thirty Pieces

An excellent kit, containing all tools necessary for making ordinary repairs. All tools of the highest grade and fully warranted. Case is heavy waterproof canvas with harness leather retaining straps sewed and double riveted. We recommend this kit to the automobile owners.

Motorists were expected to carry extensive tool kits, such as this thirty-piece Vlchek example. No date is available.

Steamer automobiles. Though F. O. and F. E. Stanley resembled bookends, appearing much like the Smith Brothers who posed for the mug shots on the cough drop box, their designs were sound. In the end, however, steam lost out because it was bulky and technologically limited. Electrical cars, which accounted for almost 40 percent of the market in the early 1900s, were rejected for want of power and because their range was limited between recharges.

Bodies and frames were no early bargain, either. No matter what kind of powerplant resided under the bonnet, that hood fea-

tured massive, oil-soaked leather straps that held it in place, or exterior hinges almost the size of a fist. Trim molding might be anything but most often was oversized and of brass, wood, or bronze.

Automobiles had improved considerably by 1914 when the Dodge brothers introduced the first mass-produced, all-steel bodied car. Enamel paint that could be oven dried and interchangeability of parts became popular in the teens and greatly accelerated mass production.

America's First Automotive Shop

Before the century turned, gasoline engine designs shared a certain unreliability that would convert their bothersome bark to blissful silence in a split second. One of the first persons to realize the potential for fixing sick cars was an ambitious salesperson named William E. Metzger. Metzger lived in Detroit and was a partner in the Metzger-Huber Bicycle Shop. Caught up like most other Americans in technological matters, he went to London in 1895 to gate-crash the world's first automobile show. The sights and sounds of Asters, Mercedes, Panhard-Levassors, and Thornycroft Steamers made his transoceanic junket worthwhile.

Metzger became recognized as America's first automobile dealer by opening a showroom for Wintons and other makes in 1898. His shop was on Jefferson Avenue in what would become known as the Motor City. The single room was part display area and part repair facility. The first sale was that of a Waverly electric to Newton Annis, a Detroit furrier. A year later, Metzger staged Detroit's first auto show. Simultaneously, Metzger moved to larger quarters. Selling and repairing cars had a future, as hundreds of fellow car dealers sprung up in Metzger's wake.

Metzger reserved an entirely separate area in 1899 for servicing cars; not just Wintons, mind you, but any of the several makes that passed or happened to stall in front of his shop. Metzger's foresight concerning repair, notes the Detroit Public Library's respected National Automotive History Collection,

Lambert friction-drive vehicles were produced from 1901 to 1916, though this tourer is a 1908 model.

Right, this cover from a very early catalogue illustrates the advantage of the interchangeable Snap-on concept.

makes him America's first automobile shop owner. Who was the first mechanic? No one is sure, but the title could belong to a friend from up the street by the name of Byron "Barney" Everitt. A Canadian by birth, Everitt was associated for a number of years with Metzger after operating his own carriage-trimming business.

Research in automotive archives shows that Metzger, who spent much of his life in automobiles, beat out a spacious Studebaker shop and showroom, which opened in 1885 in Chicago, for the title of first automobile-service facility. The "Studebaker Repository," as it was called, really was a service station, but not for cars. The facility performed wagon and coach repairs, but could not have serviced Studebakers, since the first such car bearing that name was one of only twenty electric runabouts constructed in 1902. The Studebaker brothers had prospered by building wagons in nearby South Bend, Indiana, since 1858.

Happily, Metzger realized some personal prosperity from his venture. Sales soon required him to add four more floors to his two-floor dealership, and he helped found several car companies, including the Rickenbacker and the E.M.F. The "E" in E.M.F. was Barney Everitt, whose credits also include building bodies for the first 10,000 Fords and convincing Fred and Charles Fisher (founders of Fisher Body, but not the "F" in

William E. Metzger, America's first automobile dealer and the first person to set aside space for maintenance of the cars he sold.

J.W. Lambert, an executive with Buckeye Manufacturing, was motoring down the streets of Ohio City, Ohio, in 1891 in a three-wheel car of his own design.

E.M.F.) to move from Ohio to Michigan to perform their craft on the bestselling curved-dash Oldsmobile. (Incidentally, Studebaker bought and resold much of E.M.F.'s production before taking the company over in 1911. The first gasoline-powered automobile with a Studebaker nameplate appeared the following year.)

New makes of cars began popping up all over the country. Cañon City, Colorado, saw the birth of the St. John in 1903. The Sunset steamer, crafted in San Francisco, was produced one year, in 1904. Sioux Falls, South Dakota, offered the Silent Sioux in 1909, Atlanta boasted the Primo in 1910, Kenosha, Wisconsin, was the birthplace of the Nash in 1911, and Los Angeles prepared for the Poppy Car in 1917. As the years went along, different cars shared similar Buda, Continental, Lycoming, or other mass-produced powerplants. In all of North America, some 1,640 different nameplates would appear above familiar—and not so familiar—radiators through the years.

No matter who serviced the early machines, their work was cut out for them: There simply were no established mechanical standards. Different cars—and different versions of the same car—relied on different fasteners, they seldom shared the same

E-M-F vehicles such as this 1910 touring car sold for $1,250. The "M" in the nameplate belonged to William Metzger.

A True Horseless Carriage

One of the first things you notice about Dr. Richard Scharchburg's 1905 "Curved Dash" Oldsmobile is its size. If you visualize one of today's lawnmower engines when thinking of the single-cylinder Olds, your perspective is all wrong, says the current owner.

"This engine is huge," Scharchburg says, noting that the power plant is mounted front-to-back beneath the seat. The crank is 90 degrees to the engine and, therefore, crosswise to the body. "The cylinder alone weighs nineteen pounds, the flywheel weighs sixty pounds, the piston is five inches in diameter and six inches long." In contrast, the two back brakes, affixed to the rear wheels, are only an inch

Professor Richard Scharchburg's 1905 Curved-Dash Oldsmobile. A runaway best seller, vehicles such as this put thousands of horses out to pasture. Courtesy Richard P. Scharchburg

wide and about seven inches in diameter. The entire car is suspended by two immense springs that run from the rear axle along the side of the body to the front axle. The only other spring is elliptical. It connects the front axle to the steering tiller.

What's the vehicle like to drive? "Scary," reports the director of the GMI Alumni Foundation Collection of Industrial History at General Motors' GMI Engineering and Management Institute in Flint, Michigan. "Imagine being in the seat of a horse and buggy. Now take away the horse. You're high off the ground, there's nothing between you and the road, and you can watch the wheels go round a few inches from your feet."

Happily, if you're patient, the early Olds will reward you by starting. Before turning the crank, though, you must oil everything, turn down the grease cups, and turn on the gravity-feed oiler that drips into the cylinder. There's a compression release and a spark retarder which need tending before cranking from the driver's side of the machine. Idle speed is about 500 revolutions per minute, with peak rpm about 750 and top speed perhaps thirty miles per hour. The fuel tank holds four gallons, enough to propel you about 100 miles.

Easing yourself up onto the genuine leather seat, the first thing you may notice is the lone pedal on the floor. Fortunately, it's a brake. The accelerator is a "speeder"—a lever that lets you increase or decrease the amount of gasoline headed toward the combustion chamber. There are three other levers, one for spark, one for compression, and one for the clutch. The transmission is planetary, with two speeds forward and one reverse. High-speed forward is direct drive. Under way, you need fear nothing except being passed by a dog on an uphill climb. Because the transmission is planetary, you can shift into low from high and usually make your way to the crest—if you're patient. With a

wheelbase of about sixty-seven inches, the car turns in a small radius.

The professor acquired the Olds in the summer of 1993. Black trimmed in red, the car was running at the time but the kerosene lamps and the floormat, among other things, were wrong. Nevertheless, Dr. Scharchburg was able to drive his new purchase home after acquiring and installing a new set of tires. The only interruption between the former owner's home and the Scharchburg garage was provided by a cop. He attempted to ticket the new Olds owner for traveling five miles per hour in a forty-five mile-per-hour zone. The professor was able to explain away the lack of license plate, title, or registration, but the law-enforcement officer let him go only after he promised to take side roads on the way to his Grand Blanc, Michigan, residence.

Dr. Scharchburg is no dabbler. He purchased a 1927 Star several years ago, and he and his family performed a ground-up restoration on the machine. "But it was too modern," he indicates. "The Curved-Dash Olds truly represents the bridge between the horse and buggy and the automobile. It is indeed a horseless carriage." The latest owner knows all the facts about the Olds, and he is very loyal. Sold from 1901 through 1905, some 19,000 models were built and 300 exist today. It was a moderately priced machine at the time, selling for about $850. What about reliability, Doc? "Reliable? A Curved-Dash Olds ran from New York to San Francisco in 1904, and in 1905 another Olds was driven from Lansing, Michigan, to Seattle, a distance of 4,400 miles."

But what was the determining factor, the intangible, that caused the professor to write out a check for an eighty-nine-year-old car with an exhaust note like the noise made by a cement mixer ? "My wife was out of town," says Dr. Scharchburg.

crude chain or belt drive, they rolled along on dissimilar wheels, and their engines varied in size and complexity from single-cylinder stump-pullers to multicylinder behemoths. Tool quality was quite uniform—it was substandard. Socket wrenches were made of cheap, tubular metal that quietly folded under human torque while other tools were stamped out of unalloyed iron. Equally frustrating was the small range of available tools, leaving even the best and most flexible mechanic unable to reach crucial nuts or bolts without partial disassembly.

America's First Automobile Race

Back in 1895, the same year Heinz introduced canned baked beans and Kellogg began to offer flaked breakfast food, the first U.S. automobile race was staged. A Chicago newspaper, the *Times Herald*, laid out a course that stretched fifty-two miles up the Lake Michigan shoreline as far as the city of Waukegan. The race, held on Thanksgiving Day, attracted eighty entries—but only six starters! The contest was run over muddy streets covered with a fresh blanket of snow. Ten hours and twenty-three minutes after the start, a Duryea driven by a dazed J.F. Duryea crossed the finish line, having averaged just over five miles per hour. At least one driver dropped out from the cold and from the beating he suffered as the steering tiller battered him whenever his vehicle hit frozen ruts.

Other races deserve mention. The first car race on a track was staged at Narragansett Park, Cranston, Rhode Island, in 1896. Some 40,000 persons attended, pointing up a closed track's obvious advantage—admission could be charged. Six gasoline and two electric cars raced in several heats for prizes totaling $1,000. The first long-distance race went 500 miles, from New York City westward to Buffalo. Held in 1901 under the Automobile Club of America, the event was won by David Wolfe Bishop in a French Panhard. He averaged fifteen miles per hour to finish ahead of eighty other starters. The contest stopped on consecutive evenings in Poughkeepsie, Albany, Herkimer, Syracuse, and Rochester!

The *world's* first automobile race had taken place in 1894 in

Left, Charles Duryea sits in the actual car that won America's first automobile race, run in a snowy Chicago in 1895.

Ransom E. Olds. He came up with a best-selling car, the single-cylinder Curved-Dash Oldsmobile, in 1901.

France. Europe was at least as taken with the automobile as were folks all across the U.S., but circumstances made it almost seem that America had been created for the automobile. In England, looked on by many Americans at the time as their mother country, progress lagged due to tight laws and population density. Until late 1896, for example, a person with a flag had to precede every British motorist as a warning to local residents! In rugged places such as Austria, mountains would curb highway construction until well into the twentieth century. And in what we now call the emerging world, colonialism, lack of materials, and lack of funds made even the most resourceful mechanic a pedestrian.

Despite a lack of developed roads, interest in speed continued.

The Stanley Brothers of Steamer fame.

The Stanley brothers drew worldwide attention when Fred Marriott drove a streamlined Steamer to the unheard-of speed of 127.66 miles per hour along Ormond Beach, Florida, in 1906. Though only about 80,000 automobiles existed in the entire United States at the time, this kind of publicity made car nuts out of anyone who could read. Small wonder that several Detroit-area builders and designers formed something called General Motors in 1908 and believed it would succeed. One of the principals, William C. Durant, would soon build a Chevrolet, named after Louis Chevrolet, who for several years ran a successful team of Buick racers.

Automotive Ingenuity

Wherever there were wheels there was imagination. An English inventor by the name of Hubert Cecil Booth put together the world's first mobile vacuum cleaner in 1901. Sizeable and therefore housed in a motorized carriage, it was designed to suck dirt into the waiting canister via 800 feet of hose. One can only imagine waiting for hose-bearing workers to pull up at the curb, then making sure kids and pets steered clear of the big nozzle. Also in 1901 in the United Kingdom, the City and Suburban Carriage Company of London erected

the first multi-story parking garage. Up Vermont way, a physician began the first successful coast-to-coast drive in the summer of 1903. Automobiles were everywhere, doing everything, and they were here to stay.

In 1901, Oldsmobiles outsold all other makes. That same year, a Swiss named Charles E. Guillaume created an alloy of nickel and steel. The alloy would eventually show up in automotive tooling, alongside such innovations as the pneumatic tire (1895), the automotive speedometer (1896), the rear-view mirror (1896), the magneto (1897), the tire valve (1897), the alkaline battery (1900), and mass-produced metal nuts and bolts (1900).

With each succeeding year came innovation. Autocar, an Ardmore, Pennsylvania, manufacturer, offered the first circulating lubrication system in 1904. In 1907, Detroit carmaker Northern, became the first to equip its products with left-hand steering. B.F. Goodrich introduced the cord tire in 1910, about the time that tread patterns began to show up on car tires. Hudson designed and constructed the first sedan in 1913.

Although each of these technical breakthroughs was important in and of itself, it would require the further addition of a Michigan farmboy to incorporate these and other breakthroughs into the most widely known cars of all time. That person was Henry Ford.

Born while Abraham Lincoln was president, Henry Ford got into the automobile business because he didn't want to spend the rest of his life on his father's spread just outside Detroit. Ford found farm life monotonous, but he took great pleasure in maintaining his dad's McCormick reaper and working on other machinery and equipment that, at the time, was state of rural art. In contrast, this young man with the active and inquisitive mind tried at least one other talent—watch repair—before he thought of building an automobile.

"Automobile" may be imprecise. Ford used four bicycle wheels and called his first car the Quadricycle. Designed on the back of a sheet of organ music while Henry was employed by Detroit's Edison Illuminating Company, the first Quadricycle engine was completed on Christmas Eve, 1893. The handwheel of an old lathe served as the flywheel while a discarded piece of pipe became the single cylinder. Ordinary house current was used to make a spark from a wire dangling above the piston. Ford ran the device for one minute and then put it aside to begin work on a two-cylinder version. Three years later, in 1896, a completed Ford moved Henry, wife Clara, and son Edsel around Detroit. Ford chained and locked the car to a lamppost when he stopped to prevent Detroiters from trying the Quadricycle on their own. Some things haven't changed.

Henry Ford's Formula

Unlike many of his amateur peers, Ford quickly sold his first machine and began work on another—and another and another. During the period 1896-1908, Ford made several interesting and comparatively reliable automobiles. He gave them letters rather than names, producing the a Model "A" in 1903, a Model "B" and a "C" in 1905, followed by the "N," the "K," the "R," and the "S" before unveiling the Model T late in 1908. This vehicle would separate Ford from the many other manufacturers who were on the verge of automotive success:

This Stanley racer set a world's record for speed in 1906 by steaming down Ormond Beach, Florida, at the rate of 127 miles per hour.

Fifteen million T's were sold during 19 years of production. Ford's formula was simple. His cars were low-priced, durable, and fairly easy to operate and repair.

Four years after its introduction, the Model T was being produced on a massive assembly line. The key idea here was to bring the car to the worker, rather than vice versa. Before Ford, highly skilled technicians assembled cars from beginning to end. With the assembly line, each worker had a specific, speedy, relatively simple job to do as the partially built car passed by. This was important for two reasons: It meant that semiskilled rather than skilled people could build a quality vehicle, and that assembly lines would lead to standardized parts, which in turn would lead to lower manufacturing costs. Nimble young guys earned a respectable living on the line at Ford. Eventually, a new Model T would emerge every twenty-four seconds.

Thirteen years after its debut, the Ford Motor Company was selling more than 1 million cars a year. A Ford plant was in operation in England in 1914, prior to the start of World War I. Ford was a pioneer in making vehicles with interchangeable parts, and he worked to maintain quality while producing his products for less money. The Model T offered for the 1909 model year could be had for $825 while the 1926 Model T sold for an amazing $260! Extreme wealth made Ford highly respected and somewhat strange. He put on a public show of trying to keep the U.S. out of World War I, and he was ridiculed mercilessly for his quirks and prejudices. Yet Ford was a genius as surely as was his friend and idol, Thomas A. Edison.

Ford faced two kinds of competition—cars that worked and cars that didn't. For every Maxwell or Lozier with something to offer, there was a machine like the Brush. Created in Detroit beginning in 1907, the Brush featured a wooden frame, as did many contemporary automobiles, and wooden axles—a poor choice of materials for such exposed components. "Wooden body, wooden axle, wouldn't start!" was the chant that haunted the unlucky make, which became part of a conglomerate called U.S. Motors Co., which collapsed in 1913. Other automobiles went away simply because they could not keep pace with Ford

This is a 1911 Maxwell. The make survived the collapse of the United States Motor group in 1912 and was made until 1925, when Walter Chrysler replaced it with his auto-motive namesake.

technology. For example, the unfortunately named Bug-mobile, with by-then anti-quated tiller steering, was made only for the year 1909 in Chicago before disappear-ing.

In other news during the century's first decade, Carry Nation, the scourge of saloons, took to carrying a tavern-chop-ping hatchet in 1900. The following year, President McKinley

was assassinated. Panama won independence in connection with a U.S. pledge to dig the canal in 1903, and the Wright brothers got off the ground later that same year. The first Rotary Club met in Chicago in 1905, with San Francisco's infamous earthquake shaking America's prettiest city one year later. A financial panic briefly gripped America in 1907, Admiral Robert E. Peary reached the North Pole in 1909, and the following year saw the founding of the Boy Scouts.

There were many unusual occurrences connected with the first quarter century of the automobile. A young man named

A line of early Fords in Highland Park, Michigan.

Floyd Clymer opened a car dealership in rural Colorado in 1905, selling twenty-six Cadillacs, Maxwells, and Reos in a two-year span. He was eleven years of age at the time! (Clymer spent his life in and around automobiles and motorcycles on the West Coast; he raced, he wrote, he published.) Crowds of thousands gathered in places like Nashville to watch Model T's and other cars successfully climb the steps of state capitols and public libraries. And an early craftsman in Massachusetts by the name of Curtiss built and sold his first car to a deadbeat; he went to the buyer's house and took back his creation, thereby becoming the first recorded repo man.

The Pursuit of Quality

For every unusual individual or event there were dozens of professional people committed to automotive quality. Among the best was Henry M. Leland, the man who created Cadillac's still-sparkling reputation. Leland was the first person to achieve scrupulous parts interchangeability, which he proved in Great Britain in 1908 by disassembling three Cadillacs, scrambling the pieces, then rebuilding the cars so that they ran without a flaw. Leland also knew what the public wanted—the 1912 Cadillac was the first automobile to feature electric starting and electric lights as standard equipment.

Henry Leland, shown here in 1915, made Cadillacs synonymous with quality by insisting on interchangeable parts.

Right, Actress Mabell Norman is dwarfed by this 1913 Rolls-Royce Silver Ghost. The spacious English cars were so popular among the well-to-do that Rolls-Royces were assembled in the U.S. from 1920 to 1931.

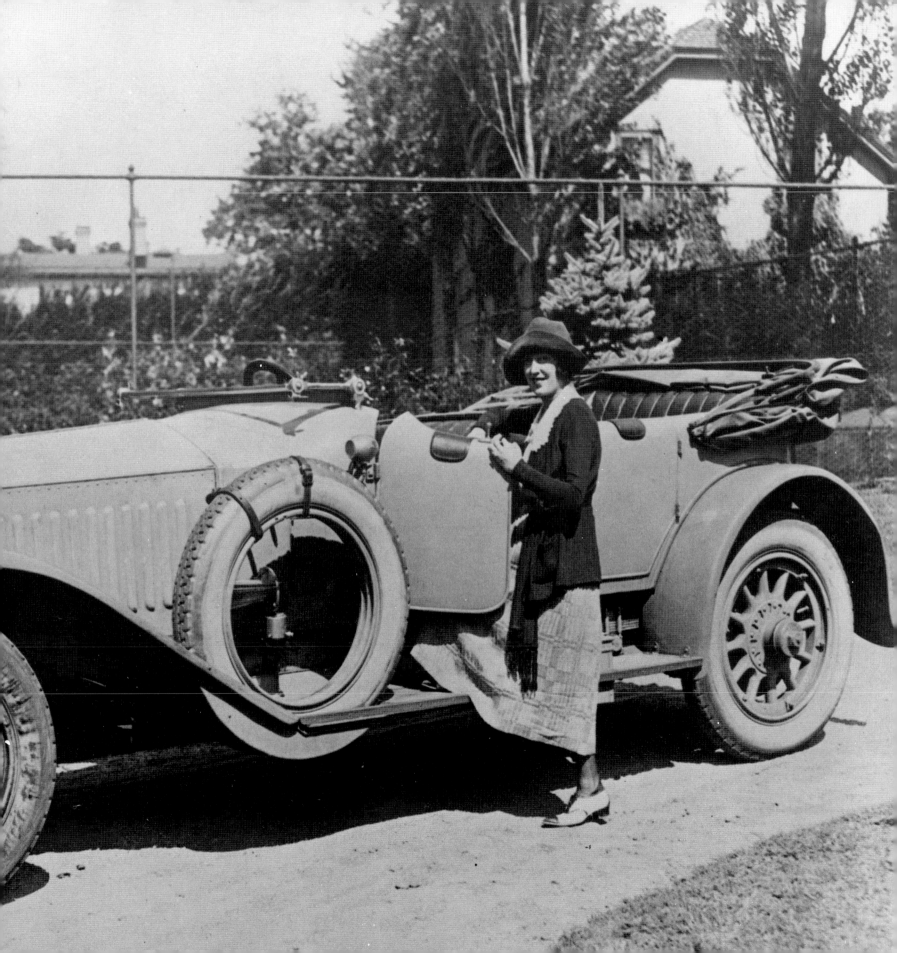

Barney Oilfield

William C. (Billy) Durant made Buick America's most popular car, then founded General Motors.

Left, Barney Oldfield, seen here in 1909, was America's first widely known racing driver. Henry Ford once told Oldfield that the two had made each other famous. "But I did a much better job," Oldfield remarked.

Car-mad Americans staged the first twenty-four hour race in Philadelphia in 1907 and made the Vanderbilt Cup race in 1910 on Long Island the largest sporting event in American history to that time. The following year, the first 500-mile race was staged in Indianapolis. Race driver Barney Oldfield was at least as famous as heavyweight boxing champ Jack Johnson, whom he once raced and beat. Barney began his career as Henry Ford's riding mechanic. He won in Fords before being hired to run the Peerless "Green Dragon." A thundering single seater without fenders, the Peerless would roll into town with Barney at the wheel, offering to race anyone driving anything handy. He once raced and beat Lincoln Beachey in an early Wright biplane. Though he never won the Indianapolis 500, Oldfield placed fifth in the 1914 and 1916 events and was the first driver to turn a lap on the 2.5-mile oval at more than 100 miles per hour.

Oldfield also was the first racing driver to become a household word, as a whole new batch of car cliches entered the language. "Get a Horse!" was uttered every time a driver stopped to peer beneath the hood. The running board became a popular perch for police and for machine-gun wielding, Prohibition-era gangsters a few years later. Chassis were the medium for every kind of vehicle, from ambulances used throughout World War I to ladder-bedecked fire trucks to carriers of the mail. Cars even became movie stars: Mack Sennett sent the Keystone Kops rolling insanely into the paths of more trolleys than anyone could count while Laurel and Hardy and Buster Keaton did battle in and with automobiles for Hal Roach.

Early Fords and Their Keeper

Early Fords held a surprise for the unsuspecting operator. Successfully turning the cold engine over with the hand crank meant that the car might suddenly jump into one of its two forward gears. Crank in hand, the operator heard the engine catch and immediately lunged against the radiator to prevent being run over.

Resourceful owners stuck a brick in front of one wheel to avoid a head-on collision with their Model T the moment the motor caught.

That's just one anecdote from mechanic Stanley M. Sibo, who may have one of the world's great jobs. Stan keeps the priceless cars running at Dearborn's Green-

Stanley M. Sibo wrenching on a 1938 American Bantam roadster at Dearborn's Greenfield Village.

field Village. The thirteen vehicles, mostly Fords, are as old as 1923 or as new as 1949. The oldest is a Model T, coated in black as were all T's built between 1914 and 1925. What's it like to drive the famous name with the four-cylinder, 175-cubic-inch, L-head engine? "The difference between a 1995 Ford and a 1923 Ford is this: The new car drives you, but you have to drive the old one," he says.

Sitting behind the wheel of a classic Ford, an operator immediately notes a greatly simplified instrument panel in the middle of the dash and a lever atop the steering quadrant. That lever is the accelerator. Pull it down to accelerate, pull it up to decelerate. The pedals on the floor include a brake that acts on the transmission bands and a clutch pedal. Pushed all the way in, the clutch is in low gear. All the way out is high. Half way is neutral. The planetary transmission, Sibo notes, let Hollywood's silent filmmakers have some visual fun. "You could go forward one second and backward the next. It's hard on your neck, and it's not good for the car, but it's funny to see."

Sibo has at least one other Ford from the past in his presence. He's restoring a 1907 Model "S" for a collector. Stanley notes that the 1923 T evolved into a much more complex piece of equipment. For example, the S featured a transmission that was open—you peeled back the floorboard, and there were churning gears. By '23, the T's tranny was safely encased, and the gears were bathed in oil from the crankcase. Starting the earlier model must be accomplished from the rear, tugging at the flywheel. That makes getting run over impossible, but it also makes the brick under one wheel even more important. The model Sibo is restoring once started, lurched out of a garage, and crossed a street before banging into a tree. The radiator still shows a big dent.

Fortunately, beginning in 1919, Fords also offered electric starting. That made the little choke-adjustment wire running from the engine to the left side of the radiator unnecessary; Sibo uses the hand crank on the 1923 these days to set the timing. "Fords were basic cars," he says. "New owners got a book that told them everything they needed to know. A set of simple tools came with each car." Sibo says the 1907 Ford was a great improvement over Henry's Quadricycle, a replica of which he drove in the summer of 1994. The Quad's only suspension was semi-elliptical springing in the front. The seat was a board with a pad on it and steering was accomplished with a tiller. His chance to drive the reproduction came during the fifty-fifth annual Old Car Festival at Greenfield Village.

One other thing: How did Sibo get one of the world's best wrench jobs? He's experienced and he's good. "I graduated from Ferris State College, and I served four years in the Navy as a machinist's mate, doing engine work. I did lots of quarter-mile and oval-track engine prep as a machinist for Jack Rousch (a maker of speed equipment). Those were mostly Ford engines, but I had a small-block Chevy, a '69 Camaro, that was an eleven-second street car. The gas mileage was awful.

"My dad worked for G.M. in sheet-metal mockup. We got experimental stuff for next to nothing—bushels of fuel injection systems and rods and pistons for pennies a pound. You had to guess what was there. I got this job after working for a company that did on-site servicing at the (Henry Ford) museum. I've always liked antiques."

Stanley Sibo's is an example of a life unique to an industrial society: As he improves or maintains the machines, the machines continue to fascinate and provide for him. Not a bad deal.

From before World War I until the onset of the Great Depression in 1930, work on the first coast-to-coast highway took place. The road was named the Lincoln Highway by its businessmen backers, who felt that no one could oppose a road named after the Great Emancipator. The 3,384-mile thoroughfare began in New York City and ended in San Francisco. Today it is known as U.S. Hwy. 30. Those who endorsed the idea of a nationwide road were sometimes rewarded by having it run through their cities. (for example, Goodyear Tire & Rubber in Akron, Ohio). Other transcontinental routes were undertaken after the First World War, including U.S. Hwy. 40 from Baltimore to the West Coast and the Dixie Highway from Lake Superior to Florida. Cars needed places to run.

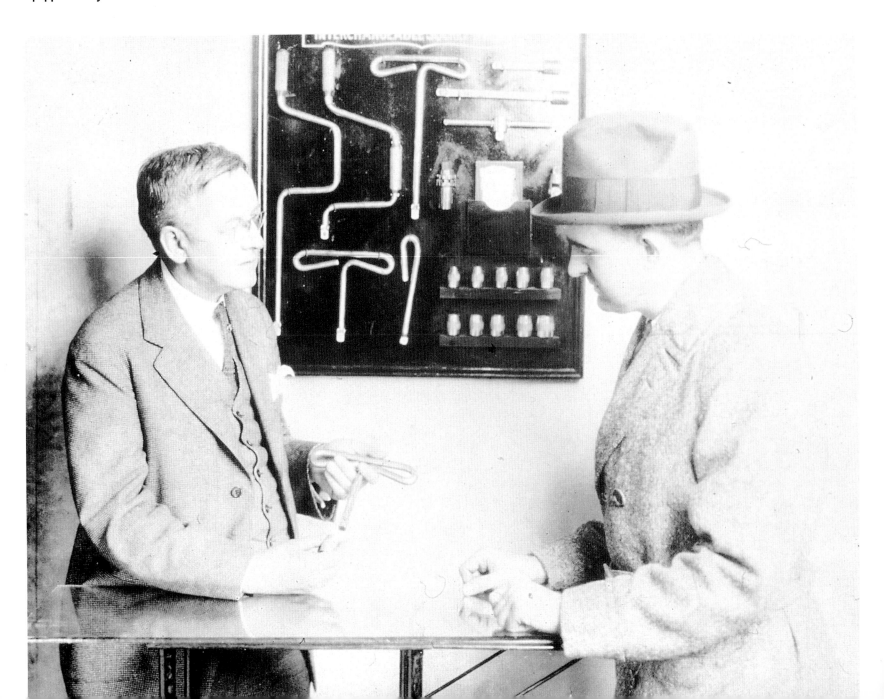

William Seidemann circa 1920, when he and Joseph Johnson began to discuss ways to improve hand tools.

For Cadillacs, Chevrolets, Dodges, Fords, Oldsmobiles, Packards, Studebakers, and other major makes, a huge and growing aftermarket industry sprang up. Persons who did not intend to get completely soaked bought supplementary canvas side curtains for their vehicles. Owners who wanted to perform their own maintenance were sold oil and grease, as well as saddle soap for the upholstery. Other aftermarket items included larger-capacity radiators, race-car bodies, the Kant-Creep Inside Tire Patch, theftproof spare-tire carriers, fuel gauges and speedometers, touch-up paint, and, for the shade-tree mechanic, an array of tools.

By 1913, car owners with a yen for aftermarket items, but without tools or know-how, could get help at a drive-in service station. The first such site was opened by the Gulf Refining Company at Baum Boulevard and St. Clair Street in Pittsburgh. The station remained open twenty-four hours a day, selling just thirty gallons of fuel on the first day in business. From this humble beginning came stations selling gasoline, oil, and other items but accurately described by the term "service." With the first of many automobile service companies formed in 1915, and more than one million cars manufactured domestically in 1916 (1,525,578, to be precise), the need for service was a growing one.

Joe Johnson's Idea

It's not quite true that all tools during the early service years were junk. Such respected names as Mossberg, the firearms manufacturer, created quality products for Fords and other cars. But since there were hundreds of automobiles from which to

Joe Johnson, whose interchangeable socket idea spawned today's billion-dollar Snap-on Incorporated. This photo was taken at about the time the company was founded in 1920.

choose, and since hubs on Whippets and hubs on Hudsons seldom were the same size, lots of people were making lots of tools in a big hurry. Equally important, the tools weren't always well thought out. A separate wrench configuration for every nut and bolt on a car was heavy to lug around and a sizeable investment. Was there a better and more efficient way for mechanics to fix the contemporary automobile?

There was, and a very young man by the name of Joseph Johnson was among the first to imagine it. Johnson was born in

Milwaukee in 1894, about 300 miles west of Henry Ford's Dearborn home. Like many Midwest metropolises, Milwaukee rumbled with industrial production in the early part of the century. Johnson secured full-time employment at the age of fourteen, serving a foundry as an errand boy. He worked three years as a stock clerk at a tannery, realizing while still in his teens that he had an intuitive way with numbers. That realization led him to a rubber company as a cost clerk. Johnson then spent five years with a maker of cardboard boxes. As World War I reached its armistice, Joe joined the American Grinder Manufacturing Company, initially as an expediter and then, in 1919, as the twenty-five-year-old manager of the wrench and tool division.

Johnson wasn't necessarily well versed in handling wrenches and tools, but he was a clear and practical thinker. This son of Norwegian immigrants realized that American Grinder had made a sudden switch to tools because government orders for their grinders and pumps related to World War I were dwindling while tools were an ongoing need among car owners and professional mechanics. Johnson and the company purchasing agent, William A. Seidemann, soon became friends—they were both managers in a shaky company, and Johnson was only a year younger than Seidemann, who had grown up on a farm north of Milwaukee.

Over lunch, packed before daybreak and hauled to the plant in pails, the two shared their dreams. Those dreams no doubt included car talk, as one may have wished for the latest, fastest Stutz while the other dreamed of rewarding himself with a Pierce-Arrow. But they talked of other things, particularly company products. American Grinder sought to ride out a brief but intense postwar recession by producing socket wrenches. These one-piece units cost from forty cents to $1.80, depending on size and handle design. Joe Johnson, cautious himself with a buck, realized that mechanics purchased a new handle every time they purchased a different socket. There were interchangeable pressed-tube sockets earlier, but Johnson would be the first to mill them out of solid bar stock. Why not sell technicians only five different handles and then interchange ten socket sizes to obtain the benefits of fifty wrenches?

Encouraged by Seidemann, Johnson approached the vice president and works manager of American Grinder with his idea. "Five do the work of fifty" of the conventional socket wrenches, Joe said, articulating what would become Snap-on's first motto. The senior executive explained that the company was tooled up to make individual socket wrenches and that Johnson's idea would result in the sales of fewer, rather than more, products. The would-be inventor left his superior's office knowing that he had given American Grinder right of first refusal to his proposed line of tools, which he named "Snap-on." Now all he had to do was convince someone besides his buddy Bill that the quality interchangeable idea was legitimate.

Johnson's lunch pail a few weeks later was heavier than usual. He closed the door to Seidemann's office, dug out his lunch, and then dumped a set of five handles onto Bill's desk. Seidemann hefted the handles, envisioned snapping various sockets on and off, and quickly agreed to help Johnson fabricate a complete set of sockets in a welding shop that belonged to a Johnson relative. The following Saturday, Johnson and Seidemann pulled on old clothes and went to work. All day long, and for several weekends afterward, they used crude equipment to mill Johnson's sockets out of bar steel. They drilled holes, bent iron, and stamped stock numbers entirely by hand. At long last, they had their product.

The Nameplates Fade

While the first Snap-on tools were taking shape, many lesser lights in the automobile industry were fading. Respected names like Argonne, Biddle, Cameron, Chalmers, Champion, Cole, Driggs, Fergus, Fox, Haynes, Lozier, McLaughlin, Owen Magnetic, Phianna, Standard, Templar, and Wasp failed to survive the immediate postwar period. The Cole was the first automobile with balloon tires, the Fergus was the first car to offer a rubber-mounted engine, and the Wasp came with a bronze St. Christopher medallion on its dashboard as standard equipment. Larger car companies adopted innovations that worked, then sold parts to smaller manufacturers. Small automakers tried to justify modest production and higher prices with superior assembly.

Yet for all their problems, American carmakers had it easier than their counterparts in Europe. Gasoline has always been less expensive and transported more readily in the United States. (It was not until the Mideast crisis of 1973-74 that Great Britain looked for, and found, oil deposits in the North Sea.) The British weren't necessarily sold on auto transportation as a way of life—the speed limit in England was twenty miles per hour until 1930. And on the Continent, when there was an emergency, auto transportation sometimes lost out. For example, the beginning of World War I saw the French military commandeer Parisian taxis in order to haul soldiers to the front.

There were fewer than 460,000 cars registered in the United States in 1910. Five years later there were 2.3 million, and five years after that there were 8.1 million. Henry Ford realized early that workers had to be paid well in order to afford the products they were making. In 1914, the same year as the first commercial passenger flight, between Tampa and St. Petersburg, Henry hiked wages of Ford assembly personnel from $2.40 for a nine-hour day to $5.00 for an eight-hour day. What economic and social effects would such numbers have on the country? Consumers and carmakers alike expressed relief at the end of World War I, looking hopefully toward the decade that would come to be called The Roaring Twenties.

Two

BETWEEN THE WARS, 1920-1940

*O*pportunism has acquired a negative connotation, and perhaps that's too bad. It has come to mean taking advantage of circumstances without regard for consequences. In the case of Snap-on, Joseph Johnson's opportunism has resulted in rewarding and fulfilling career employment for thousands of Americans in Wisconsin, other areas of the U.S., and abroad. Equally important, it greatly increased vehicular productivity, it reduced downtime, and it maintained the income of untold hundreds of thousands of mechanics and vehicle owners. Were Joe Johnson alive today, he would be amazed at the mushrooming effect of his opportunism—especially in view of the fact that he and William Seidemann created their first set of

Two Chevrolet salespeople await customers in a dealership in 1928. Chevys at the time were price competitive with Fords but lacked the Model A's quality.

A very early Snap-on sales vehicle, probably a Model T Ford, and probably in Milwaukee in the early 1920s.

A Snap-on display, probably at a county fair. Note that Fords merited special attention, since they were well made and by far the most popular vehicles at the time.

Joe Johnson dictates a letter. Calm and practical, Johnson gave time, money, and effort in later years toward a number of charitable undertakings in the Kenosha area.

tools and discovered they were all but broke.

Johnson and Seidemann, described respectively in an early history as "affable" and as "a down-to-earth plugger," spent their last few dollars on photos that went into 2,000 brochures telling all about the new tools. The brochure boasted that Snap-on Tools, as they were called from the start, were unique because "Five do the work of fifty" conventional tools. Five handles and ten sockets were all the two had, so they struck a deal with a traveling tire salesman who covered Wisconsin. That first Snap-on salesman called on independent garages and automobile dealerships, showing the lone set of

tools and leaving behind a brochure. Five hundred C.O.D. orders soon filled his pockets, and he returned to Milwaukee. Meanwhile, the founders were making a second set of tools for a second traveling salesman. The results were similarly spectacular.

Each of the two identical tool sets contained five handles: the Long Speeder, Rim Brace, Long Tee, Short Tee, and Offset. The ten sockets ranged in size from 7/16in to 7/8in and the square drive of the handles and sockets was 1/2in. The 1/2in square drive has remained basic in the Snap-on line down through the years. So has the square end of each handle, which was fitted with a spring-and-ball friction grip over which the sockets could be snapped. From this feature comes the product name and the trademark.

The Snap-on Wrench Company

Armed with orders (but neither tools nor money), Joe and Bill found a well-connected attorney. The lawyer turned up two major local industrialists willing to invest, and incorporation of the Snap-on Wrench Company took place on April 10, 1920. Johnson was a mere twenty-six at the time, Seidemann twenty-seven. Joe and Bill each borrowed $500 so that they could purchase some of their own stock. It was understood that they would pay for the balance of their holdings out of future earnings. A 2,500-square-foot shop was rented, machinery was leased, stock was stored, and production began.

Who would sell the product? Neither Johnson nor Seidemann was an experienced peddler, and the fellows who handed over the many C.O.D. orders had previously committed to selling vehicle tires. Besides, their territory covered only Wisconsin, and the new corporation wanted to go nationwide. The founders ran an ad in Chicago newspapers, attracting Stanton

Stanton Palmer was Snap-on's first full-time salesperson and later became the first president of the newly incorporated company. He and fellow salesperson Newton Tarble came up with the idea of selling directly to mechanics.

Palmer, a factory sales representative. They showed Palmer their wrenches, which he thought enough of to pretty much drop whatever else he was doing. Palmer in turn hired Newton E. Tarble, a printing salesman, and the two salesmen agreed late in 1920 to be the exclusive sales agents for Snap-on. Palmer and Tarble bought out Johnson and Seidemann's original financial backers. Stanton Palmer so impressed the other three that he was soon elected the company's first president. A

decision he made very early in his career with Snap-on riveted his partners to the way he did business and was to affect the corporation to this day.

Shortly after joining Snap-on, Palmer and Tarble went to the National Hardware Convention in St. Louis. The two may have thought they would sell thousands of wrench sets to the big jobbers, but the same kind of thinking shown Joe Johnson by the American Grinding

Newton Tarble served Snap-on as a salesperson before buying into the fledgling firm and becoming an officer in the new corporation.

exec was displayed by the hardware companies. To coin a contemporary phrase, Stanton and Newt were blown off by the big distributors of automotive accessories.

Returning to Chicago on the train, the two felt so strongly about the product that they decided to sell directly to mechanics. Yet they feared the wrath of the mighty parts jobbers, whose lines of distribution they might someday need. To shield the fledgling firm from possible jobber wrath, the two came up with a sales organization for Snap-on tools that they called Motor Tool Specialty Company. Equally important, the sales organization's different name would let them sell other tools of lesser quality without associating those tools with Snap-on. Mighty as Motor Tool may have sounded, it began with just two people. They ordered 200 sets of wrenches and hit the road, calling primarily on auto mechanics. Stan and Newt sold 650 sets in their first sixteen days and never looked back.

Stanton Palmer, by all accounts, was a legendary salesperson. He knew intuitively that the tools clanking in his briefcase were premium products, and he treated them as such when pitching mechanics. Palmer acquired a rectangle of green, pool-table felt, which he reverently spread before a group of shop people prior to laying out handles and sockets for display. It became known as "The Magic Green Cloth." He ran a file across a han-

dle to prove finish strength as he passed tools around his circle of listeners. Picking a mechanic who was obviously dazzled, he would ask that person to collect the names

of all assembled, as well as a $2 deposit from each. Palmer took the list and the deposits, pledged to return with their tools in a few days, and was out the door, on the way to the next garage.

The two founders resigned their positions at American Grinder and went to work full time at their new venture. Johnson and Seidemann quickly realized that the harder they worked the

of these sets were accepted and paid for, despite the months of delay in filling the orders. All four principal, it seemed, were committed to the professional hand tool business.

Why the Twenties Roared

The 1920s were a relentless period marked by bad booze, wacky stunts, and the nameplates of dozens of long-forgotten cars. The United States, because of the devastation in Europe from World War I, got a jump worth several years in automotive production and technology and took full advantage of the situation. After the tense time of the war, the world hoped for better things. Devices and inventions now taken for granted came along, from nitrocellulose lacquer in 1921 to the aerosol spray can in 1926 to hard-water soap in 1928. Hydrogen welding, which would have an effect on automobiles and many other products, was perfected in 1924. Meanwhile, Henry Ford established additional auto-assembly plants in Australia, France, Germany, New Zealand, Spain, Japan, and in the suspicious new Union of Soviet Socialist Republics.

Women were given the vote in 1920. The following year, a U.S. Congress frightened by foreign radicals curbed immigration. Coal-mine strikes cost thirty-six lives in 1922, the same year *Reader's Digest* was founded. Lee De Forest showed the first sound-on-film movie in 1923, and in 1924 Native Americans were made U.S. citizens due to their bravery in World War I. The Scopes Monkey Trial, concerning the teaching of evolution, took place in 1925. Employment at Snap-on exceeded sixty employees by 1926, the same year that Congress established the Army Air Corps. A year after that, Charles Lindbergh landed in Paris, and Amelia Earhart duplicated Lucky Lindy's feat in 1928. The St. Valentine's Day Massacre in Chicago ended the decade for several mobsters in 1929 as Wall Street stocks and bonds soared before plummeting.

The shape of automobiles became much more homogeneous during the 1920s. As the decade began, most cars were still open—only upscale machines such as the Marmon and the

more they fell behind. So Bill Seidemann stopped off at a nearby mission, recruiting marginal men at fifty cents an hour in the hope that they would put in at least an hour's worth of work before wandering off. Full-time help was scarce, but within six months Johnson and Seidemann had produced enough Snap-on sets to fill the C.O.D. orders taken before the company was formed. Virtually all

Packard offered solid hard-tops. By the end of the ten-year period, all cars featured sedan styling, unless ordered specifically as convertibles. Duesenberg introduced hydraulic brakes on all four wheels in 1920 (rear-wheel only brakes had seemed good enough until traffic and high speeds made quick stops desirable). An early American effort at streamlining a car

15¢ for the finest Wrench Built!

Chevrolet Snap-On set $5. Thirty-six wrenches to work with, but only three to carry.

The price was right for this 1920s Chevrolet tool kit.

body was the *Golden Submarine* built on a Miller chassis for racer Barney Oldfield. The all-enclosed aluminum shell made the racing car resemble an egg and afforded such poor visibility that Oldfield flipped the machine after running into a trackside ditch.

Half of all U.S. cars in the early 1920s were Model Ts, and American auto production exceeded the remainder of the world combined. European manufacturers went in two directions. Major makers such as Austin in Britain and Fiat in Italy followed Henry Ford's lead by offering inexpensive cars for the masses. In contrast, huge automobiles from Rolls Royce in Britain, Hispano-Suiza in Spain, Voisin in France, and Isotta-Fraschini in Italy featured the work of talented, independent coachmakers. The small cars were slow, simple, and made to run around town. The big machines were huge, fast, and in the case of one Rolls-Royce model was offered with everything from ostrich hide upholstery with ivory buttons to a dashboard made of polished rosewood. Speaking of wood, frames of ash or spruce were common.

Wood was the most common substance used to make wheels as the 1920s got under way. Artillery-style wheels, made up of about a dozen straight, sturdy, polished- wood spokes, were seen on European cars prior to World War I and on American cars into the new decade. Though more capable of high speeds than the skinny bicycle wheels they succeeded, wooden wheels didn't seem to be the ultimate solution. Henry Ford eyed Europe's pricey wire wheels with their individual, adjustable nipples, and ordered wires on his Model A Ford welded to the rim and painted rather than polished. Pressed-steel wheels also became common in the 1920s.

Strides were made in tire technolgy, with hard and narrow clincher tires, which used beads to lock into channels on wheel rims, giving way to soft-riding balloons. The wider balloons were produced initially by Firestone in the spring of 1923, for reasons of safety; narrow tires frequently caused the driver to lose control when the car crossed railroad or interurban tracks running parallel to the roadway. Also, narrow tires could not always safely ease onto a paved road from a dirt or gravel berm. Narrow wheels and tires and a high center of gravity could be deadly combinations as speeds increased. And speeds did increase—there were no limits between cities and towns until after World War II!

Americans continued to fiddle and fine tune, often with startling success. From the start, Snap-on offered a range of tools, all of the same high quality but with more handles and ratchets and wrenches in some kits than in others. As early as 1923, the "No. 101 Master Service Set" provided the automotive technicians with 330 combinations. So thorough was this set that it was advertised for work on all makes of cars. The company simultaneously accommodated those who worked on trucks or tractors: The "No. 202 Heavy Duty Set" was a basic approach and sold for a mere $8 in 1923.

The company's first patent was secured in 1923. It covered a spring-loaded ratchet adaptor, a wonderful mechanism. Tool collectors have made this one of the most sought-after collectibles in existence, a rare honor in view of the fact that most hobbyists seek only old woodworking tools. American industry took note of Snap-on tool quality, the result being a separate catalogue to address the folks in charge of tool cribs, beginning in 1935.

Snap-on's Grand Growth

The four men who would shape the youthful company complemented each other's skills. Stanton Palmer was the senior among them; he provided early financial stability and overall financial knowledge. Newton Tarble, offered sales and marketing skills, later outlined in a book, *Plan Your Work and Work Your Plan*. This salesman's guide remains an excellent tool for today's struggling salesperson. Joseph Johnson was the idea man—the inventor and the innovator. William Seidemann had a great deal of manufacturing knowledge and a range of mechanical skills. "They were," says a longtime Snap-on executive who recently retired, "a perfect team."

With Palmer installed as president, Johnson became vice president and treasurer, Tarble vice president and general sales manager, and Seidemann secretary. Johnson spent the early 1920's making dozens of trips between Chicago, home of Motor Tool Specialty, and the plant in Milwaukee, before moving briefly to the Windy City. He and Palmer orchestrated an incredible expansion (a dozen branches had opened and were selling aggressively by 1922) while Tarble sold and Seidemann somehow increased production to meet demand. Branch managers

William Seidemann as he appeared for his Snap-on company badge.

Below, those who missed their Snap-on representative when he called could always purchase tools from a branch office such as this one. On the eve of the Great Depression there were twenty-six branches in the U.S.

were selected and trained in twenty cities. They in turn recruited salespeople, who peddled tools and sent ideas for new implements from mechanics back to Chicago and Milwaukee.

"The mechanics buy wrenches in Philadelphia just like they do on Automobile Row in Chicago," an excited Newton Tarble told Stanton Palmer over the phone after a long day of selling. "Selling Snap-ons direct to garage mechanics is the only way we can hope to get volume." Palmer agreed, endorsing recruitment of branch managers and opening of branches in city after U.S. city. The level of acceptance of the innovative tools was excellent. The difference between good sales and great sales proved to lie in the quality of managers recruited. Especially strong managers and, therefore, receptive markets, could be found in Boston,

New Double-End Boxockets With Heads at 15° Angle

STRAIGHT handle Boxocket Wrenches with heads set at a 15° angle to make them especially good at clearing obstructions while providing long leverage and the advantage of a direct pull.

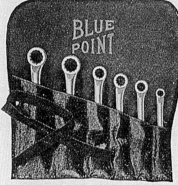

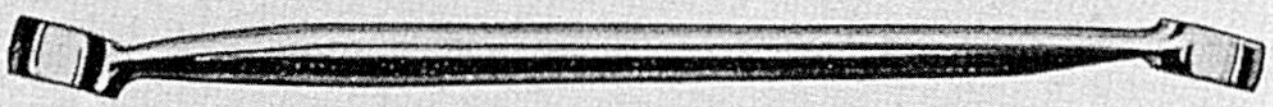

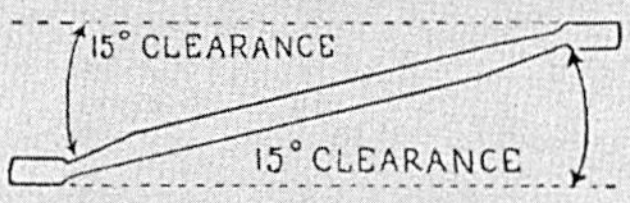

15° CLEARANCE
15° CLEARANCE

This illustrates the type of all numbers, showing the 15° angle of clearance. Double broached hexagon openings, made of Chrome Vanadium tool steel, carefully heat-treated, cadmium plated finish.

No.	Openings	Length	Each
XD-1416	⁷⁄₁₆″ and ½″	8¼″	$1.20
XD-1618	½″ and ⁹⁄₁₆″	8¾″	1.30
XD-1820	⁹⁄₁₆″ and ⅝″	9¼″	1.35
*XD-1922	¹⁹⁄₃₂″ and ¹¹⁄₁₆″	9½″	1.40
XD-2022	⅝″ and ¹¹⁄₁₆″	10″	1.40
XD-2024	⅝″ and ¾″	11″	1.45
*XD-2226	¹¹⁄₁₆″ and ¹³⁄₁₆″	11¼″	1.55
*XD-2526	²⁵⁄₃₂″ and ¹³⁄₁₆″	11½″	1.65
XD-2428	¾″ and ⅞″	11¾″	1.70
XD-2830	⅞″ and ¹⁵⁄₁₆″	13″	1.80
XD-3032	¹⁵⁄₁₆″ and 1″	15⅜″	2.25
XD-3034	¹⁵⁄₁₆″ and 1¹⁄₁₆″	15⅜″	2.30
*XD-3134	³¹⁄₃₂″ and 1¹⁄₁₆″	15⅜″	2.30
XD-3440	1¹⁄₁₆″ and 1¼″	15⅜″	2.50
XD-3640	1⅛″ and 1¼″	15⅜″	2.55
XD-4244	1⁵⁄₁₆″ and 1⅜″	15⅜″	2.85

(*) Not carried in stock. Supplied on special order only.

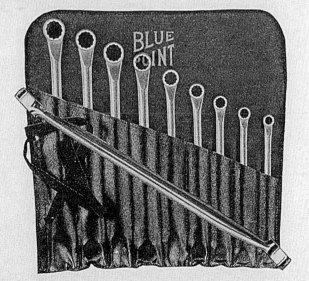

XD-9 Set—Consisting of 9 wrenches in popular sizes, Nos. XD-1416, XD-1618, XD-1820, XD-2022, XD-2428, XD-3032, XD-3034, XD-3640 and XD-4244. Tools only. Net..........$16.90
XD-9K Set—Above tools in No. 7-C leatherette kit. Net..$17.25

Boxocket Wrenches Are Safety-First Tools

Dwarf Boxocket Wrenches
[Trade Mark]

THESE are the smallest wrenches of the Boxocket line. The handles are short so that they can be used in close places, the openings are double broached, like the larger Boxockets, for free operation where turning space is limited. Each end has a different sized opening and is offset, as illustrated, to clear obstructions. Made in the most popular and needed sizes. Make easy work of a lot of close-quarter jobs, including generator, universal joint and carburetor work, servicing cover plates and manifolding systems.

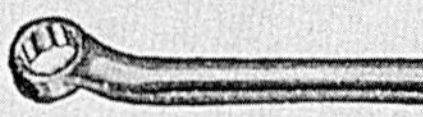

No.	Opening	Length	Each
XS-1214	⅜″ and ⁷⁄₁₆″	4″	$0.90
XS-1416	⁷⁄₁₆″ and ½″	4½″	.95
XS-1618	½″ and ⁹⁄₁₆″	4¾″	1.00
XS-1820	⁹⁄₁₆″ and ⅝″	5″	1.15
XS-2024	⅝″ and ¾″	5¼″	1.30
XS-2224	¹¹⁄₁₆″ and ¾″	5¾″	1.55

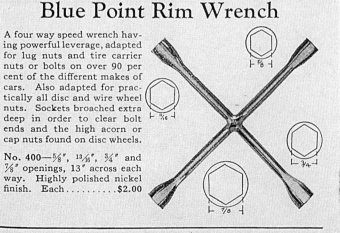

Dwarf Set in Kit Bag

The above six sizes of Dwarf Boxocket wrenches put up in a leatherette kit bag, giving you a mighty handy outfit of these popular and much-used sizes. No set of wrenches could give you more practical service— you should have the complete set.

XS-6 Set—Wrenches only, ...$6.85
XS-6K Set—Complete in No. 1-C kit bag.......$7.05

Blue Point Rim Wrench

A four way speed wrench having powerful leverage, adapted for lug nuts and tire carrier nuts or bolts on over 90 per cent of the different makes of cars. Also adapted for practically all disc and wire wheel nuts. Sockets broached extra deep in order to clear bolt ends and the high acorn or cap nuts found on disc wheels.

No. 400—⅝″, ¹³⁄₁₆″, ¾″ and ⅞″ openings, 13″ across each way. Highly polished nickel finish. Each..........$2.00

Ask Salesmen About Special Boxockets

A filling station in Ohio, about 1923. Filling stations became service stations when the fellows who manned the pumps began to fix cars. Note that a gallon of Peerless gasoline sold for twenty-three cents. *Scott Benjamin*

Chicago, and, by 1927, in French-speaking Montreal.

By 1923, Snap-on offered special tools for all of the well-known makes and some that weren't so common—including Dort, Gardner, Gray, Jewett, Jordan, Kissel, Lexington, Moon, Overland, Peerless, Reo, Star Car, Stearns, Stephens, and Velie. An eleven-piece set for a Buick offered the mechanic sixty possible combinations from six sockets and five handles. The "Special Service Set for Ford Mechanics" sold for $14.85, with an extra $3.00 for a metal carrying case. A tool tray, a small cabinet, or a leather pouch, the latter designed to slide under the vehicle's front seat, also were available.

Much can be learned from a Snap-on catalogue, even the modest, sixteen-page initial version from 1923 that fit in a shirt pocket. The service set for Ford mechanics supplemented the simple, lower-quality tools that came with the car. As early as 1925 the company warned of cheap imitations while, in 1927, the catalogue featured both Snap-on and Blue Point tools (the latter primarily open-end wrenches, plus chisels and punches). By 1928, the variety of Snap-on tools precluded the need for a make-by-make breakdown. That same year, the $12, twenty-pound Mechanikit metal tool box, complete with its own Yale lock, was shown maintaining its shape beneath the weight of a massive Jordan sedan.

Mechanics could even come clean with Zowie Soap Tabs—Alka-Seltzer-sized pieces that were reputed to make even the

An early Shell Oil filling station. A brick facade and a tiled roof smack of permanence, in contrast to today's no-frills, self-service facilities.
Scott Benjamin

dirtiest hands sparkle. Gib McCreery, a former senior Snap-on executive, used to tell a funny tale about Zowie. The product was pressed sawdust soaked in alkaline and was subject to great expansion when wet. As a young salesman on the East Coast, McCreery once had a trunk full of Zowie that he attempted to deliver during a driving rain. The trunk was leaky, as you might guess, and when McCreery opened it in front of his customer, the cardboard Zowie boxes burst open and the product immediately increased in size by 100 percent! "Zowie!" probably was the mildest thing McCreery yelled on that long-ago afternoon.

Wrenches, tool kits, pliers, soap—everything Snap-on offered proved popular to mechanics everywhere. Perhaps that is why the company established a New York City office in 1927 to deal with leading importers and dealers abroad. Nearly a decade had passed since the end of World War I, and U.S. companies like General Motors were buying existing plants such as Vauxhall in Britain and Opel in Germany. Even more important, the average European could increasingly afford one of the hordes of small Austin, Morris, Renault, or Fiat machines being produced there. Every car owner not only was a potential customer for a mechanic but was a potential mechanic, as well.

Pittsburgh Snap-on salesperson W. G. Finnie no doubt had mechanics in mind when he called on the Wilson Motor Company one day in the 1920s. Finnie found that radio station WJBV had scheduled a remote broadcast from the car dealership, but that the singer scheduled to perform had failed to show. Setting aside his sample case, Finnie delivered a pair of songs to a small but eager audience—then took phone-in requests for five more! There's no mention of his sales success that day, but Finnie's guileless offer to save the day represented the kind of attitude the company sought for calling on the nation's automotive technicians.

From the beginning, Snap-on products were being constantly upgraded. Boxocket wrenches, introduced in 1926 and a company trademark, were less apt to slip off the nut or round off its corners under heavy use. They offered the handle length of an open-end wrench and the opening of a socket wrench, and they were designed to accept a variety of handles. It became entirely possible to sell the same product repeatedly, in the same garage, month after month, since good mechanics were in demand and switched jobs frequently. The guys peering under the hoods in the summer weren't always the fellows performing preventive winter maintenance—which became standard by the late 1920s as antifreezes improved, the quality and viscosity of oil stabilized, and batteries lasted longer.

Snap-on salespeople were kept carefully abreast of the latest product developments. At a sales confab in the 1920s, an executive was expounding on the fact that Snap-on was the first company to make high-quality sockets by milling them from bar steel. One of the company's branch managers, half asleep but still scribbling notes, got home later and reviewed what he had written. He alerted his sales force to the fact that Snap-on was using a remarkable new alloy called "Millfrm Bar Steel." Almost immediately, the company began receiving requests to share the source of Millfrm Bar Steel, a rare and superior substance!

Expansion, Depression, Contraction

A major name was created in 1924 when the old Maxwell firm was taken over by Walter P. Chrysler. He produced an extremely popular four-cylinder machine in 1925 that was soon joined by an Imperial Six, then DeSoto, then Plymouth. Chrysler took over Dodge in 1928. At the Chevrolet Division of General

The first Chrysler. Though the profile isn't striking, such items as balloon tires, high-compression heads, and hydraulic band brakes quickly made it a popular vehicle.

Motors, the company recovered from a mechanical disaster in 1923 by recalling and destroying a new "copper-cooled" model with a radiator that poached the engine. By 1927, the year of the first drive-up mailbox, introduced in Houston, Chevy sold more than one million cars a year to become the country's most popular machine. The automaker went to an overhead-valve, six-cylinder engine in 1928 but was displaced atop the sales heap in 1929 and 1930 by Ford's new V-8 Model A. This V-8 60, as the 60-horsepower motor was known, enhanced Ford's reputation due to its extended life.

No matter the make of car, a highway trip from the late 1920s on would reward driver and passengers with wonderful scenery, fresh air, and Burma-Shave rhymes. A former insurance man in Minneapolis helped develop the brand of brushless shaving cream, then hit upon the idea of selling it on small, consecutive, red-and-white signs placed along the right of way. Some 7,000 signs with rhymes like *Train wrecks fewer/Reason clear/Fireman never hugs/Engineer/Burma-Shave* dotted the landscape for more than thirty years. Always in good taste, the rhymes disappeared only after television and much higher speeds overwhelmed the clever little interruptions.

The late 1920s and early 1930s saw the automobile transformed from a flivver to a work of art in America. General Motors under Harley Earle may have gotten things started with a series of brilliant styling exercises on the 1927 LaSalle chassis. Smaller manufacturers in particular who wanted to compete for the eye of the public turned to custom-body coachmakers with

The new 1928 Model A Ford, with 50A Sport Coupe body, is displayed by movie star Delores Del Rio. One million were sold in the first sixteen months of production.

names like Brewster, Brunn, Darrin, Dietrich, Holbrook, and LeBaron. These firms built bodies by hand for an audience that would dwindle as the era matured. Auto production in 1932, the Great Depression's worst year, would dip to the lowest level since 1918. The few who were buying and could afford luxury did not always want to show off a handmade car.

Joe Johnson spent the latter part of the 1920s promotiong the Snap-on line to "smokestacks," the large automobile manufacturing plants in the Detroit area. He made the acquaintance, too, of people in the production and service divisions of the car companies. Bill Seidemann concentrated on making contact with industrial buyers. Small wonder that, by 1930, only ten years after the company's start, sales reached $1,835,679. And since salespeople were paid by commission and were responsible for their own expenses, the company could operate with a high degree of efficiency—until industrial layoffs became widespread. There were twenty-six Snap-on sales branches and 300 salesmen in 1929.

Automobiles registered in the United States numbered 23,035,000 by 1930, the first full year of the Great Depression. Registrations in Canada, where Snap-on maintained sales offices in Montreal, Toronto, and Vancouver by 1932, exceeded one milion vehicles. One year before that, in 1931, Snap-on Tools of Canada Ltd. became the company's first international subsidiary. Yet the economies of both countries—and the rest of the carmaking world—were bad and getting worse. The Great Depression was a technical school for auto owners and mechanics—destitute people learned to keep cars running with baling wire, fistfuls of grease, watery gasoline, and little else. The fact that Snap-on grew to thirty-two branches in 1933, with a sales force of 350, says a great deal about product demand, though the company lost $39,790 in 1932.

Earlier, in a classic case of unfortunate timing, Snap-on began construction, in January, 1930, of a 60,000 sqare-foot factory and general office on the outskirts of nearby Kenosha, Wisconsin. Kenosha was Wisconsin's third largest city, with a population of more than 40,000. On Lake Michigan some sixty miles

Suitcase to Cellular—the Radio Telephone

You there—the driver meandering down the highway while chatting on the cellular phone. Think the appliance hooked to your ear is some new-fangled device? You couldn't be more wrong.

The first successful installation of a radio telephone in an automobile took place in June 1919. Michael J. Kollins, writing in the December 1993 edition of *Wheels,* the journal of the National Automotive History Collection, notes that "radio-phone equipment" at the time was capable of maintaining communication with another station at distances of up to twenty miles. Those of you who experience fade driving from one side of a major city to the other will realize that the technology hasn't improved all that much.

The big advantage of today's cellular technology is size. An illustration accompanying the Kollins article shows a fellow behind the wheel, wearing earphones, and turned so that he can adjust the controls on his radio-telephone in an area behind the front seat. And what a radio-telephone! The size of the average suitcase, it probably outweighed a big-boned Black Lab. There are dials, buttons, and various other controls.

The technology first took off with Guglielmo M. Marconi, who in 1894 sent radio signals three-fourths of a mile via electrical waves. The brilliant, studious Italian was granted an English patent based on the theory that the range of wireless communication increased in proportion to the height of the antennas. Early wireless devices proved their worth by receiving distress calls from ships at sea.

The first American president to communicate by means of radio was Woodrow Wilson. He spoke with members of his cabinet, who were in Washington, D.C., from a ship on July 4, 1919. Commercial radio programming began in the fall of 1920. Detroit's WWJ and Pittsburgh's KDKA started regular broadcasts. Motorola pioneered commercial radio in automobiles in the 1930s.

Police in the U.S. began using radio car phones in the 1920s. Motorcycle cops had to wait several years for technology to produce a two-way radio that was not affected by the cycle's electrical system. Before that, motorcycle police received transmissions but were unable to reply to their dispatcher.

Just outside the new Kenosha plant in the 1930s lay cornfield stubble. Today, the home office and production facilities are surrounded by a pleasant neighborhood.

Right, this French-Canadian Snap-on dealer plied the roads of Quebec in the 1930's. Canada has been a strong Snap-on market for almost as long as the company has existed.

Left, founders Johnson (right) and Seidemann. They may just have realized that their new Kenosha plant would have to be paid for with Depression-era dollars.

Above, this spotless 1930s Ohio General Motors dealership used and promoted its Weidenhoff tune-up equipment. Snap-on purchased Weidenhoff Corporation in 1956.

Numerous A&W stands were constructed in the shapes of lighthouses, Indian heads, and root beer barrels. The nickel-a-glass "Natural Temperance Drink" was a popular item during Prohibition. *A&W Restaurants, Inc.*

Right, engine analysis equipment in a state-of-the-art Chicago-area garage around 1930.

depression reality. Top stars of the decade included Claudette Colbert, Betty Davis, Vivian Leigh, Clark Gable, James Stewart, and Spencer Tracy. Gable in particular was a car nut, being photographed frequently at the wheel of machines most people only dreamed of.

What else happened? The Empire State Building opened in 1931, World War I veterans marched on Washington seeking bonus pay for their service in 1932, and President Franklin D. Roosevelt ordered all banks closed in 1933. In a headline with a more modern ring, U.S. troops pulled out of Haiti in 1934. The following year, comedian Will Rogers died in an airplane crash, and the Social Security Act passed Congress. Boulder Dam was completed in 1936, the same year Margaret Mitchell published *Gone With the Wind.* Joe Louis won the heavyweight boxing championship in 1937, as auto and steel labor unions were winning their first big contracts. A federal Minimum Wage Act came along in 1938, and in 1939 America declared itself neutral in the war in Europe as it armed the Allies and rearmed itself.

One of the funniest auto-industry stories from the 1930s lies almost buried today. In developing their Airflow design, Chrysler engineers in 1933 wondered just how aerodynamic their conventional cars really were. A 1933 DeSoto was put through its paces in a wind tunnel and found to generate 20 percent less drag when presented trunk first to the blast of air! This confirmed studies done in 1931 and 1932 at the University of

Snap-on added a line of open-end wrenches and a series of chisels and punches in the early 1920s and called the new line Blue Points.

Michigan. American cars tested in a wind tunnel there had 47 to 57 percent of the drag of a flat plate of similar frontal area. Handsome as some early 1930s designs might have been, they simply weren't all that efficient.

The decade, along with settling in in Kenosha and running an overextended company, went ahead without Snap-on President Stanton Palmer. He died in 1931 and was replaced by E. William Myers.

Below, A Miller powered by a V-8 Ford from the early 1930s. The driver is Indianapolis 500 veteran Lou Fageol. Despite the beauty and power of these machines, the Great Depression forced Miller into bankruptcy in 1932.

The bank appointed Myers to the position because Snap-on was deeply in debt to him and his company. Myers owned Forged Steel Products, a Pennsylvania firm that made pliers

Another shot from the Weidenhoff files, this photo showing a circa-1930 Indy car being analyzed by Weidenhoff technicians.

marketed by Snap-on. The new boss wasn't always popular, having to make penny-pinching decisions throughout the 1930s that resulted in layoffs and other unpleasantries. In fact, he and Newt Tarble never really saw eye to eye and Tarble, the largest stockholder, left the company in 1935 (though he remained a director).

Myers also had difficulty with union organizing, which took place in many industries during the 1930s. He fired a Snap-on

organizer, and this firing led to a six-week strike. Arbitration resulted in the organizer being rehired and in eventual union representation by what is known today as Local 34 of the International Association of Machinists and Aerospace Workers. Myers also attempted to merge Forged Steel Products with Snap-on Tools. The result was a merger and then a rapid unmerger, as both sides felt it was in their best interest to part. Though they merged for good in 1945, Myers would not see it. The man who made the tough, depression-era decisions that kept the company going died of a perforated ulcer in February 1939 at the age of only 47.

The company used two successful selling techniques to rise above competitors such as Blackhawk, Bonney, Cornwall, Husky, Truth, and Sears during the thirties. The first was the development of a "Needs List." One salesman had been writing up "dream orders" with mechanics in his territory. "Let's dream up a list of tools you'll need when you have some money," he said. Rogers (Rod) Palmer, Stanton Palmer's son, was named vice president and general sales manager in 1935. He took each customer's dream and turned it into a Needs List; in addition to being a record of admitted future needs, it also became a route list, purchase record, and a basis for territorial sales statistics, including more accurate sales forecasts. The Needs List kept mechanics thinking about—and, to some extent, buying—Snap-on offerings.

The second technique involved extending credit to mechanics. This was a hazardous practice in lean times, but it proved to be a policy that created much good will. Obviously, only a brave—or desperate—company could offer credit to guys who didn't know how much longer the garage or the plant could keep them on. In fact, Snap-on itself came very close to closing its doors for good during the 1930s economic tailspin.

Better Tools

Despite the monetary crisis that seemed to have no end, real advances were made in the 1930s. By the middle of the decade, Snap-on tools featured better steel, thinner socket walls, better heat treating, superior plating and finish, and 1,600 different tools in the combined Snap-on and Blue Point lines. Snap-on pioneered the master 1/2-inch drive, the midget 9/32-inch drive, the ferret 3/8-inch drive, the heavy-duty 3/4-inch drive and the extra heavy-duty 1-inch drive. By 1936, Snap-on realized $2,495,000 in sales and $88,495 in net profit, the company's best year of an admittedly dismal decade. Snap-on sales guys by this time were showing up in spotless white coveralls, the Snap-on logo on one breast pocket, the Blue Point logo on the other. (The Blue Point

A 1937 Cord 812. This model was supercharged and featured front-wheel drive, but neither innovation could save Cord from extinction. Cord was the first front-wheel drive car in serious production in the United States.

A Pontiac showroom in Los Angeles, 1939.

logo was used primarily for products purchased on the outside for resale.)

The economy affected everything in the 1930s, including racing. During the 1920s, respected small automakers such as Duesenberg competed on the track against foreign racers like Peugeot and Ballot on one hand and gifted small garages such as Frontenac on the other. (Frontenac cylinder heads for Ford engines were first produced in 1918–by Arthur and Louis Chevrolet!) Harry A. Miller, a talented carburetor specialist from Los Angeles, crafted wonderful racers throughout the twenties. His cars won the Indianapolis 500 a dozen times between 1923 and 1938. He helped carry racing's flag through the depression, despite going bankrupt in 1932 and being overpowered by Offenhauser and Maserati machines just prior to World War II.

Snap-on's first venture into the world of racing sponsorship was modest and brief. The company helped fund two dirt-track cars, a Snap-on Special and a Blue Point Tool Special, that ran on bullrings in places like Brazil, Indiana, and Amboy, Illinois, during the summer of 1929. The sponsorship apparently ended when Benny Benefiel, the driver, was injured while trying to qualify for the 1930 Indianapolis 500.

Not all endorsements from well-known people involved any kind of formal relationship—Harold I. June was the chief pilot for the Admiral William Byrd expedition of the South Pole in 1935. He wrote the company to report that Snap-on tools worked wonderfully in the deep freeze at the bottom of the earth. Admiral Byrd himself added written congratulations. The year 1935 also is significant in the southern hemisphere because Snap-on opened up its first branch outside North America, in Sao Paolo, Brazil.

The best-known person to make a living with cars during the period may have been E. G. "Cannon Ball" Baker. From the teens into the 1950s, Cannon Ball crisscrossed the country, setting performance, mileage, or endurance driving records for whichever company chose to hire him. His customers included, at one time or another, Chrysler, Franklin, Kaiser-Frazer, Nash, Revere, Rickenbacker, Stutz, and Willys-Overland. Baker proved more long-lived, and much less notorious, than another wheel-man, Clyde Barrow. The thirties bank robber once wrote a letter to Henry Ford, endorsing the getaway power of the V-8 in his freshly stolen Model A. Baker and Barrow probably attracted more attention than people such as Joe Morris and his Death Dodgers, though Morris's gang of stunt drivers played in forty-two states and had offices in Cincinnati and Detroit in 1937.

Speaking of stunt drivers, the first automobile driving course was offered to high school students living in State College, Pennsylvania, in 1934. The first instructor was a brave gentleman by the name of Amos Earl Neyhart, and kids completing the course received Pennsylvania operators' licenses. To the north and east, Connecticut became the first state to issue permanent license plates. Hartford did so in 1937, providing a plain aluminum plate with black letters. The first auto license plate of any kind had been decreed by the state of New York in 1901, and the first colored tabs noting the change from one year to the next weren't introduced (by Massachusetts, to save metal) until 1942.

A few years earlier, automobile production was beginning in Japan. The first Nissan was quite similar in size and design to the British Austin Seven, featuring a four-cylinder, forty-five-cubic-inch engine. Nissan negotiated with but failed to produce a Ford but did make a number of larger cars that looked like a U.S. prod-uct, the Graham-Paige, beginning in 1937. Toyota's first car came out in 1935. It was powered by a forty-five horse, six-cylinder engine and resembled the slick but unpopular Chrysler Airflow design. Most Japanese vehicle production prior to the war, however, involved cars or trucks produced under license.

Looking in the opposite direction, several interesting developments were unveiled in Europe. Independent front suspension, which made the average car ride a lot less like a cart, showed up in the late 1920s on the Continent and soon was standard equipment on U.S. machines. Front-wheel drive was introduced by Audi in Germany and Citröen in France before the concept was seen on American Cords. And in an automobile project that was named by Adolf Hitler himself, a people's car was created in 1938 called the Volkswagen.

One huge 1930s advance in safety, though, was an idea first tried in Michigan in 1911: Paved roads were adorned with painted lines down the middle that kept drivers traveling in opposite directions out of each other's paths.

A recession within the depression struck the U.S. in 1937, the same year the company changed its name from Snap-on Tools, Inc., to Snap-on Tools Corporation. Cars of incredible beauty—with intriguing engineering and even decent reliability—bit the dust in frightening numbers. Perhaps the most handsome automobile ever designed in the United States was the Cord Models 810 and 812, created by Gordon Buehrig and produced from 1935 through 1937. The "coffin-nosed Cord" ran a Lycoming-powered V-8 engine and featured retractable headlights and a wraparound grill. The 1937 supercharged model was priced at $3,575, but only 2,320 of the front-drive Cords were made and sold in the 810/812's three model years. An example of the 812 can be seen today in the Museum of Modern Art in New York City.

The Cord's relatives, Auburn and Duesenberg, were produced in the same small plant and they, too, went away after 1937. Another Indiana make, the Marmon, suffered the same fate earlier, in 1933. Stutz, constructed across town in Indianapolis, tried to cover both ends of the spectrum by building an inexpensive six-cylinder automobile and offering a pricier version with a V-8 engine. The V-8 had two overhead camshafts and four valves

Left, a mechanic for Longnecker Motor Sales, Erie, Pennsylvania, tunes a Pontiac in the car dealer's shop in 1939. Note that the instruments being used are Suns, which now are a part of the Snap-on family of companies.

Founders Joe Johnson (left) and Bill Seidemann during Snap-on's twentieth anniversary celebration in 1940.

per cylinder. Offered in the company's Bearcat model, it was guaranteed to exceed 100 miles per hour. But not even blinding speed could save Stutz, which folded in 1935. Studebaker in South Bend narrowly survived, producing only one million cars from 1926 until 1939—less than Ford's total annual production in a single pre-depression year.

Mechanical Reliability

Throughout the 1930s' grim economic times, the doors of automobile dealerships were being kept open in large part due to the solid work of their mechanics. A 1938 federal survey indicated that the average U.S. dealer suffered a net loss of $16.71 per $1,000.00 of new car sales, but that he enjoyed a net profit of $36.83 per $1,000.00 from parts and service, for an overall profit of $20.12 per $1,000.00. That same year, Snap-on's premier offering was a 111 pound, chest-high tool cabinet that included eighty-nine socket wrench units and sixty-five Blue Point wrenches and hand tools for $234.55. This "No. 487 Super Service Set" could be viewed in the company catalogue, which numbered 136 pages. Depending on experience and in what part of

the country he was employed, the average mechanic was paid ten to fifteen dollars a week.

With his wallet so thin, the automotive technician had little time for racing, which hit a low ebb in the U.S. Wilbur Shaw, one of America's great drivers, won the Indianapolis 500 in 1939 and 1940 in an eight-cylinder Maserati. The Italian car in Shaw's hands was faster than anything on domestic tracks but ran well behind German Mercedes-Benz and Auto Union Grand Prix racers in Europe. These silver behemoths were four-wheel laboratories for engine technology soon to be used in Nazi aircraft. At the opposite extreme, midget racers were run fast and well by people like Sam Hanks, Ronny Householder, and Mel Hansen at places like Motor City Speedway in Detroit. Their cars weighed 750 pounds or less and, with their Ford V-8 60 engines, cost no more than $5,000 to build and race. Ford V-8's sat in junked cars all over the country, awaiting insertion into a midget race car.

Snap-on paid its first dividend in 1939, keeping costs contained and initiating programs such as those of field sales managers. These people, under the direction of each branch manager, worked geographical areas in need of additional sales coverage. Sales personnel went from 265 in 1935 to 556 in 1940—along with the doubling of sales volume during the five-year period. Salesmen were able to call back on each shop every two weeks, and in some cases weekly, instead of the previous four- to eight-week intervals between visits. Customer service greatly improved as Snap-on guys literally crawled beneath vehicles alongside mechanics to confirm needs and write orders. In fact, customer service became as important as product quality.

Mechanics who remained employed throughout the 1930s were fortunate. A number of those without work put in time as laborers in the federal Civilian Conservation Corps or the Work Projects Administration. The former made America a better-looking place, while the latter constructed post offices, bridges, and other infrastructure that still stands. The work of these federal programs—and the depression itself—was interrupted by rearmament. War began in Europe in 1939, and the British in particular looked to the U.S. to provide everything from troop ships to aircraft. And while there were many isola-

The Quest for Speed

"What'll she do?"

That question has been asked since before the first Stutz stuttered down the street. Men have given everything, including their lives, in search of the answer.

By the time Sir Malcolm Campbell climbed into his Sunbeam to set a record of 146.16 miles per hour in 1924, many drivers had exceeded 100. He and another well-to-do Englishman, Donald Segrave, traded the title of world's fastest human for more than a decade in the 1920s and '30s. Campbell eventually built the *Bluebird*, a car of his own design powered by a Rolls-Royce aircraft engine. Segrave set a record of 231.44 miles per hour in 1928 before Sir Malcolm ran 246.09 in Florida in 1931, 253.97 in 1932, and 272.46 in 1933. A further modified version of the 28-feet. long *Bluebird* finally ran 301.13 on the Bonneville Salt Flats with Campbell aboard in 1935.

Another Englishman, John Cobb, rewrote the record books shortly afterward. Cobb's teardrop-shaped Napier Railton was powered by a pair of aircraft engines that cranked out 2,500 horsepower. The veteran racing driver went to Bonneville in 1938 and came away with a run of 350.20 miles per hour. Just before World War II began, he returned and upped the record to 369.7 miles per hour. Cobb showed up in Utah in 1947 to run 394.2 miles per hour. One of his runs (two runs are averaged for the record) was clocked at 403.135 miles per hour, making him the first human ever to exceed 400 on land.

Cobb's record stood for sixteen years before a young Californian named Craig Breedlove came along.

A hot rodder and drag racer, Breedlove talked several large companies into sponsoring his jet-powered car, *Spirit of America*. The deep blue machine ran 407.45 miles per hour in 1963—only to be bested by more than 100 miles per hour the following year. Another drag racer, this one named Art Arfons, from Ohio, rocketed across Bonneville in 1964 to average 536.71 miles per hour. Breedlove returned in 1965 to become the first person to run above 600 mph. He averaged 600.601 miles per hour.

Gary Gabelich moved the speed farther up the peg in 1970. In his natural-gas powered vehicle, his two Bonneville runs averaged 622.407 miles per hour. The current record, set in 1983 by Richard Noble of the United Kingdom in a jet-powered car named *Thrust 2*, is 633.6 miles per hour. With the speeds so stratospheric, Utah's salt flats are the only places left where there is room to fly along the ground.

The only list as long as the record breakers is the sheet containing the names of those who died, or at least crashed trying. As early as 1928, Frank Lockhart died on the beach at Daytona while attempting to set the land-speed record in a Stutz streamliner. Both John Cobb and another land speed record holder, Sir Henry Segrave, were killed as they attempted speed records on water. Other drivers have died by other means, including road accidents, but perhaps racers William Grover-Williams of England and Robert Benoist of France suffered the most unusual end. Both joined the French resistance and were captured and executed by the Gestapo.

Packards such as this Rollston model were variously available in the late 1930s with straight-eight, V-8, or V-12 engines. Packard sold its body dies to the Soviet Union and had no luxury car to compete with Cadillac or Lincoln immediately after World War II.

tionists in the American population, that sentiment was blown away in the 1941 attack on Pearl Harbor. War was declared on Japan on December 8, 1941, and on Germany and Italy three days later.

The First Superhighway

The most important public construction projects between the wars involved highways. The Pennsylvania Turnpike Commission was established in 1937 to build a toll road across the state's Appalachian Mountains. Originally running 160 miles from Harrisburg to Pittsburgh when it opened in 1938, the divided, dual-lane road featured eleven interchanges and no cross traffic. Extended eastward to Philadelphia and westward

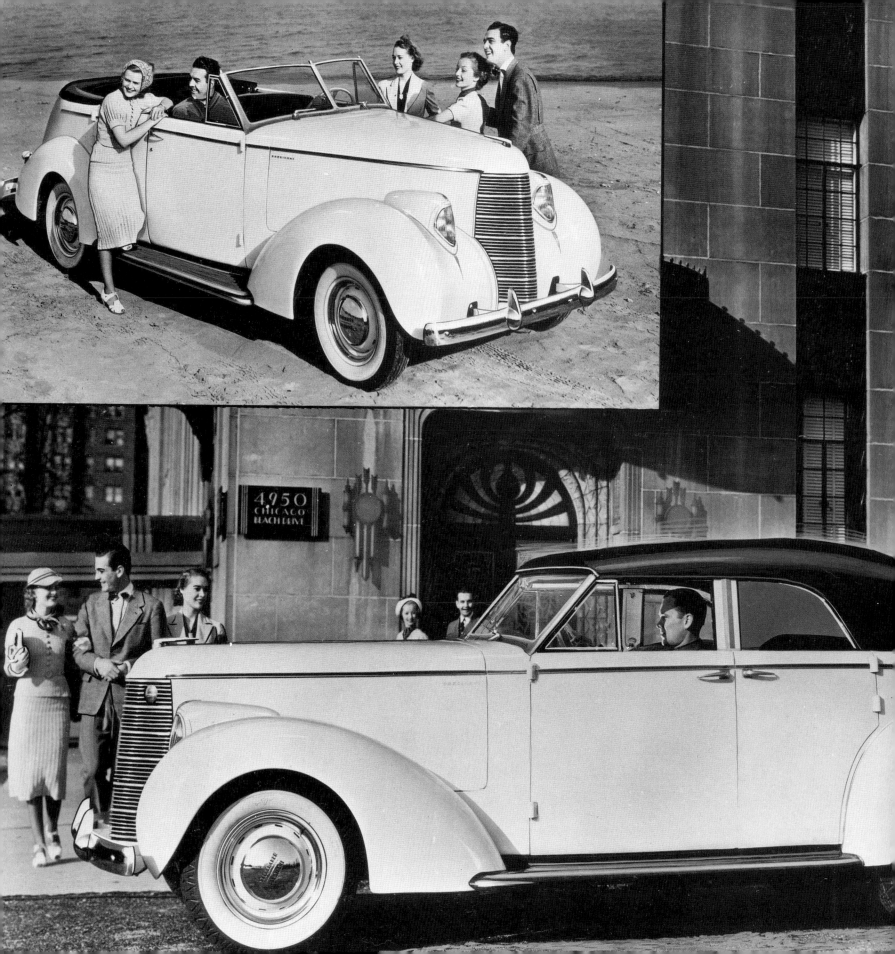

The 1938 Studebaker President featured a straight-eight engine and a rather handsome appearance. A smaller model, unfortunately, was called the Dictator at a time when Hitler and Mussolini were at the height of power.

Next page, this 1939 Pontiac Deluxe Eight Coupe is typical of cars seen on Main Street, U.S.A., on the eve of World War II. Pictured is Paula Winslow, a 1930's radio star. *Used with permission, General Motors Media Archives*

to the Ohio state line, the toll road eventually totaled 327 miles.

Germany created similar highways earlier in the 1930s and called them autobahns, but their intent was military, and they offered no quick on-off access to food or fuel. Some historians believe the autobahns were copies of a stretch of Long Island road known as the Meadowbrook Parkway, finished in 1934 and intended to connect New York City's masses to a number of Atlantic beaches. Though no one east of the Sierra Nevadas paid much attention, a stretch of street in Los Angeles called the Cahuenga Freeway also was in use in the 1930s. But the success of the Pennsylvania Turnpike would be noted and reproduced all over America beginning in the late 1950s.

Looking back, car buffs who lived through the Great Depression can recall highlights amid deprivation. Cadillac introduced its mighty V-16 in 1930, the first full year of economic woe. In 1932, as the depression bottomed out, Graham offered a supercharged car with new-fangled adornments called fender skirts. In 1934, the same year Snap-on first sold power tools in its catalogue, an estimated 200,000 American children were adrift, without homes or parents, living from one handout meal to the next. With rearmament came jobs, and with jobs came increases in car sales. By 1940, registrations totaled 27,466,000. Those new cars in late-1939 offered the buyer a shifter on the column, overdrive, hydraulic brakes, and radios, with some Packard models featuring air conditioning for the first time.

Snap-on salespeople drove newer cars with these and other amenities because their expertise was needed by agencies such as the U.S. Army Ordnance Department. A group of the company's salespeople were selected to classify and identify stock on military tool shelves. The program saved the government millions of dollars in releasing tools that had been poorly classified in various warehouses all over the country. At the factory, larger and more frequent orders from the government were received. Orders for the military delayed delivery to private parties, creating a back-order situation that would fundamentally change the basic way Snap-on did business.

Three

WORLD WAR II THROUGH THE EISENHOWER YEARS, 1940-1960

odern-day Snap-on Tools dealers should reserve a small spot in their hearts for the mother of Claude Fillingham. The Detroit-area Snap-on sales rep wrote to Kenosha in 1936 to report that his mother had given Claude and his blushing bride a new panel truck with the Snap-on logo emblazoned on its sides. Claude took his new wife on their honeymoon (which included a tour of the Indiana military academy from which Claude had graduated), then used the truck to make his calls. Fillingham's truck preceeded the concept of the walk-in van (and the independent dealer) by several years, but Mrs. Fillingham knew all along what a Snap-on dealer needed most.

Was there ever a better looking Chevrolet than the 1955 Bel-Air? In addition to handsome styling, Chevrolets were available with V-8 engines beginning with this model year.

A Snap-on dealer poses with his 1957 Dodge Route Van. America was never more car crazy than during the mid 1950's.

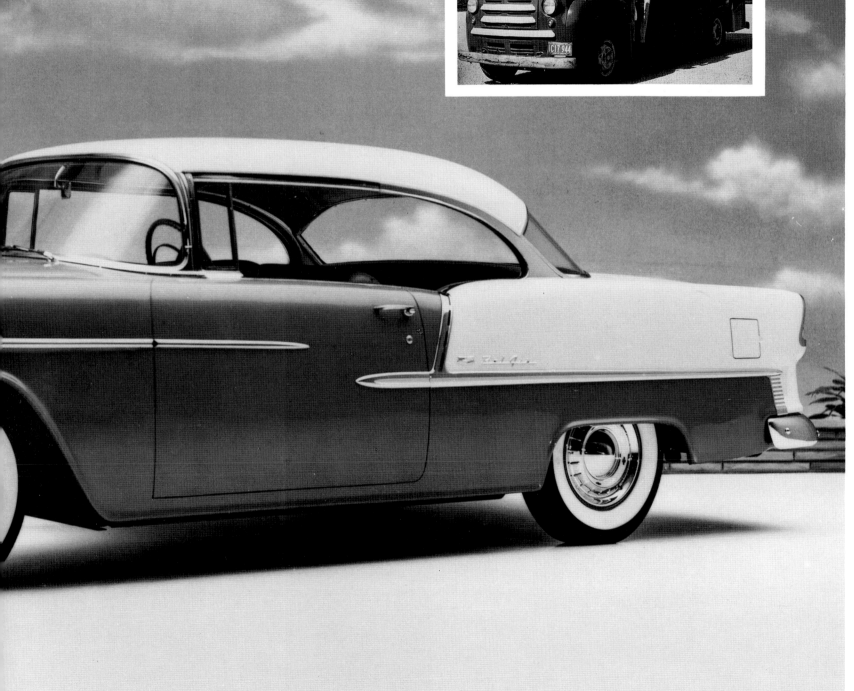

The 1941 Auto Scene

What was the market like for Claude and the many other Snap-on salespeople, working hard and keeping a nervous eye on headlines reporting war elsewhere? A study funded by the Automobile Manufacturers Association in 1941 is revealing. There were about 27.5 million cars registered in the U.S., and those cars made fifteen billion trips totaling 498 billion miles a year. More than half of the trips and three-fourths of the mileage were job related. "Necessity driving," the study called it, and it totaled 274 billion miles. As any Snap-on rep could confirm, traveling sales was the occupation recording the highest average mileage: 18,791 annually, or more than double the 1941 average per car for all drivers.

Doctors made house calls back then, and they recorded 12,932 miles from 947 trips—an average of almost three trips a day, seven days a week. Farmers at the time accounted for an amazing 17 percent of all passenger car ownership. The typical farmer averaged 12.5 miles per trip for an average annual distance of 5,750 miles. The typical wage earner drove an average of ten miles per trip (there's no indication if any of these figures are one way or round trip). Newer cars were driven an average of 9,147 miles a year, middle-aged cars were driven 7,577 miles annually, and older cars recorded just 5,479 miles. Interesting as all these stats may have been, they would soon mean very little.

More important to Snap-on folks were the huge numbers of civilian back orders created by the military's appetite for tools, which always took precedent. Such demands forced salespersons to carry ready-to-sell inventory with them wherever they called. Sold on a first come, first served basis, the tools were toted in cars, station wagons, and panel trucks. Officially, Oscar Kraft of St. Louis, with his 1932 Model A truck, owned the first walk-in vehicle used to sell tools. By 1946, Snap-on dealers were on the way to independence, with the gradual change to dealerships and franchised territories completed in 1950 in the United States and Canada. By 1954, all dealers were independent businesspeople. But we're getting ahead of our story . . .

A 1941 Oldsmobile four-door sedan. The first car with an automatic transmission (1938), Oldsmobile was for years the make on which General Motors introduced innovations.

This is the American version of the British Austin Seven, seen in 1941 with styling that was copied by Willys to create the Jeep. Called American Bantams, Austins were out of production in the U.S. by the time this military vehicle was created.

The storm that rained destruction in the Far East and in Europe for more than two years finally broke over the United States on December 7, 1941. Not many Americans knew on December 6 there was a place called Pearl Har-

bor, but they learned a great deal about the U.S. Navy's big Pacific port as they leaned toward their Crosley, Emerson and RCA console radios on that chilly Sunday evening. War had come to the United States from an almost unexpected direction, carried by an enemy determined to rule the western Pacific.

Rule Japan did, for quite a while. In fact, the Japanese briefly controlled 10 percent of the earth's surface. They realized several land and sea victories early in the conflict, though the Battle of

Midway in the middle of 1942 marked a change in fortunes for Allied powers—the number of Japanese ships lost at Midway would make defending far-flung islands difficult, then impossible. The American military, once organized, was a force to be reckoned with. It was supplied in large part by an automobile industry that moved with lightning speed. In all, automobile manufacturers turned out 4.1 million engines, 5.9 million guns, 2.8 million tanks and trucks, and 27,000 aircraft! In the end, nei-ther the Japanese nor the Germans nor the Italians stood a chance.

America's big automobile story of the 1940s decade didn't take place on the streets or behind the high walls of a proving ground. Rather, automobile manufacturers used their technical knowledge and high-speed assembly to keep U.S. soldiers and their allies better equipped than the Axis. There was little auto activity on the home front because gasoline was rationed—for a roundabout reason. The United States had more than enough petroleum, but the big concern was the rubber supply. With the Japanese occupying Malaya and other big rubber-producing areas, the federal government had to conserve the supply of raw

This guardhouse is a souvenir of World War II at the Kenosha facility. There is no record of attempted sabotage at any Snap-on facility, but that may be due to the presence of armed gatekeepers beginning early in 1942.

Mr. Lafoon appears to have converted a funeral home vehicle into a sales machine. Such ingenuity was needed to get tools to civilian mechanics during World War II.

was added. The 54,000 square feet of new space nearly doubled the size of Kenosha's original plant floor. Besides shortages of materials, equipment used night and day eventually wore out. Company co-founder Bill Seidemann and his people somehow kept the machinery together. "Chromium and other essential materials are not now available for plating purposes," the 1944 catalogue told readers. Offered instead were tools with either a brushed-zinc or oil-black finish. "We will return to our high polished chrome finish as soon as supplies are again available."

No one took the home-front auto mechanic for granted. *Chevrolier*, a monthly publication from Chevrolet, noted in its August 1943 issue that "the automotive mechanic is the service soldier of the civilian front." Indeed. An estimated six million farm familes depended on the mechanic to keep farm-to-market trucks

topped with barbed wire, a red brick guardhouse, and armed guards, as everyone was on the lookout for saboteurs. Lest someone think the company a marginal part of the war effort, General Jimmy Doolittle wrote Snap-on workers to commend them following his raid on Tokyo in 1942 "in the North American bombers you helped build." Everybody was working hard, though a small number of folks had cushy assignments. Commonwealth Edison guards in Chicago enjoyed driving around to make sure there were no members of the Axis cutting wires, and the fellows who formed the Dayton (Ohio) Funeral Escort Service led hearses to and from the church and the cemetery in cars and on motorcycles for almost four years.

Many wartime employees were women. Without previous experience, they put wonderful small-motor skills to work on ordnance assembly lines. A Delaware maker of munitions was so pleased with its female workforce during the confict that the payroll showed only an occasional male, hired for bullwork. Snap-on Tools could have met neither military nor civilian needs without the women who hung up kitchen aprons to pull on coveralls and run presses, heat-treat tools, operate lathes, pack products, and perform all the other jobs their fathers and husbands and brothers and sons performed before being called off to war.

Nothing came easily. Snap-on found that, as early as 1942, it was difficult to obtain the forgings it needed for production. A modern forge shop and an extension of the production area

Tool-selling, 1940's style. This van was well-equipped for the period, especially in view of the fact that the corporation had to live through various material shortages from the end of World War II to the end of the Korean War.

Founder Joseph Johnson, an immigrant's kid who made good, was fond of crunching numbers and puffing cigars. This photo probably was taken during World War II, while Johnson served as Snap-on's president.

Paul Russo spins out of control in the powerful Novi V-8 front-wheel drive racer at the Indianapolis 500 in 1956. That's Pat O'Connor in an Offenhauser-powered car going low to avoid the spinning Novi.

running, as well as tractors, combines, threshers, and more. Approximately 75 percent of all war workers moved by private automobile, and these machines had to be maintained because car owners had money, but there were no new models to buy. The scrapping of 2.3 million vehicles in 1943 alone placed a burden on both the vehicles that remained and those who serviced them. In all, *Chevrolier* calculated, "33,298 Chevrolet Automotive Mechanics . . . are Saving the Wheels that Serve America." So were their peers in other shops and corner stations all across the country.

If World War II had a mechanical hero, it was the Jeep. An open, four-wheel drive machine that rode on stiff suspension

continued on page 92

1955, depending on which source is consulted.

Henry J. Kaiser made a fortune in merchant-ship construction on the West Coast during World War II. He launched the Frazer, the Kaiser, and the compact Henry J., building the cars on and off from 1946 to 1955. Constructed on an assembly line in a former Ford aircraft plant in Detroit, the machines offered attractive styling but fell victim to slow sales. Willys took over the lines in 1953, moving production to Argentina after 1955. Sears, Roebuck and Co. marketed the Henry J. as an Allstate in 1952 and 1953, selling just 2,363—and receiving occasional requests for refunds, with the merchandise returned freight collect!

Is it a Kurtis? Is it a Muntz? This model is the former, powered by a Mercury V-8 and offering a fiberglass body. Just thirty-six were built in the early 1950's before Muntz took over the design.

A smaller postwar effort involved a subcompact from upstate New York named the Playboy (approximately 100 produced from 1946 through 1951) while another subcompact, the Crosley, was produced off and on from 1939 to 1952. Another small effort, in both size and money, was the Davis, a three-wheeler that could seat four abreast and was powered by a sixty-horse Hercules engine. Seventeen prototypes of the allegedly untippable car were built, but designer

A Checker cab, as produced from 1947 to 1955 in Kalamazoo, Michigan. Later models were painted to look like family sedans and were sold with either six-cylinder or V-8 Chevrolet engines.

Glenn Gordon Davis was convicted of fraud in 1949, and the project died. One of the more successful small cars of the 1950s was the two-seater Nash Metropolitan, offered in 1954 and 1955 and based on the English Austin chassis.

What, then, was the most successful independently produced car of the postwar period? Ironically, it may be the Checker, the not-yellow version of the familiar, boxy cab design made in Kalamazoo, Michigan, until 1982. Checker offered its first "pleasure car" in 1948 (though it had been making cabs since 1922). Early machines ran a six-cylinder Continental engine, which was the standard powerplant for the carmaker until 1965.

The first Checker widely offered for public sale came out in 1960. It featured the cab-style body, which debuted in 1956, but by 1965 the basic engine was a six-cylinder Chevrolet. Later Checkers offered a large and more powerful Chevy six as standard, with a Chevy V-8 standard in the premium Marathon line. As anyone who has ridden in a Checker can confirm one of its major assets was rear-seat room.

Were there other post-World War II cars? Of course. They fall into two categories: models introduced by the Big Three or foreign entries, plus numerous machines pro-

Tuckers such as this 1948 model were interesting, if for no other reason than that they were powered by flat-six, rear-mounted helicopter engines. Top speed of the short-lived Tuckers—only fifty-one were built—was said to be 122 miles per hour.

duced in tiny numbers, many with such 1930s names as Duesenberg and Stutz. And while fiberglass made body design a more reasonable proposition, no one has been able to overcome the benefits of mass production enjoyed by Chrysler, Ford, General Motors, or the leading imports.

A 1952 Allstate, sold by Sears, Roebuck and Company. This also was the Henry J, a compact car built by and named for Henry J. Kaiser.

continued from page 87

Suburbia creeps toward Snap-on's Canadian plant in this 1946 photo. The Canadian facility was fully involved in wartime production in 1939, more than two years prior to Pearl Harbor.

and skinny tires, the olive-drab Jeep was produced during the war by the Willys-Overland plant in Toledo, Ohio, and by Ford in Detroit. More than 585,000 Jeeps saw service on all fronts and at bases in the United States and Europe. After the war, Willys registered the trademark and brought out civilian versions of the quarter-ton vehicle. Jeeps often were driven without windshields, since their speed wasn't blinding but glass covered with off-road mud could easily be. These four-passenger, three-speed manual fore-

bears of today's Broncos and Blazers and Cherokees were virtually as reliable as the folks who won the war.

In all, 16.3 million Americans donned uniforms, fighting on two fronts. Snap-on's cautious rhetoric was typical of the day: There was no talk of victory until at least 1944. But the decade was not all war. In 1943, President Franklin D. Roosevelt signed the pay-as-you-go income-tax bill. Effective July 1 of that year, wage and salary earners were subject to a paycheck withholding tax. In 1946, some 400,000 miners went on strike over wages, benefits, and working conditions. Jackie Robinson became the first African American to play major-league baseball when he manned second base on opening day for the Brooklyn Dodgers in 1947. The Marshall Plan set aside $12 billion that same year to rebuild Europe. The Kinsey Report on *Sexuality in the Human Male* was big news in 1948, the year before Tokyo Rose was sent to prison for Japanese wartime broadcasts.

The conflict greatly increased Snap-on's size, importance, and reputation. The company enjoyed sales of $4.14 million, $6.9 million, $10 million, and $11.1 million, all records, in 1941, 1942, 1943, and 1944, respectively. Profits climbed, too, though there were limits put upon them by wartime federal agencies. Especially encouraging was the 1946 production year, the first full year of peace since 1940. There were fewer than 25.8 million cars on the road, and since half were more than ten years old, they needed attention. Snap-on sold $11.522 million worth of products and netted $1.44 million. The money was spread around—a retirement plan for all employees had been in place since 1943. A check stub from one of the war years showed that Joe Johnson was paid $650 a week.

Going Public, Growing Importance

As president, Johnson took the company public with its first sale of stock in 1941. A share sold for $12 at the time. With stock splits and dividends, that share would be worth about 100 shares of stock at its current market value, plus accumulated dividend. Also during his tenure, Snap-on was marked by expanding product lines, broadened geographical markets, new facilities, new products, a more sophisticated organizational structure, and a new way of making sales. By 1959, Johnson's last full year of management, Snap-on sales were $26.4 million and net profits $2.2 million. The latter figure was greater than sales volume from the founder's initial year as president. A friendly and civic-minded man, he gave of his time and his pocket to local institutions such as Kenosha Hospital and Carthage College.

Automobile racing started up again as the war ended. Snap-on employees joined area residents at the Wisconsin State Fairgrounds on Friday nights all summer as a slew of great drivers performed in midget racers, little improved since before the war. Names like Emil Andres, Tony Bettenhausen, Wild Bill O'Halloran, and Duk Nalon brought fans back repeatedly to the one-mile dirt oval. Elsewhere, stock-car racing had been staged on the beach at Daytona since the 1930s, with NASCAR, the National Association of Stock Car Auto Racing, crowning Red Byron its first champion for the 1948-49 season. Out on California's dry lakebeds, vets and other tinkerers scavenged war-surplus parts and fabricated their own designs to increase the popularity of a pre-war notion, hot rodding.

Indy after the war attracted a number of winners, and one of the great losing race cars of all time. The Novi V-8 was a supercharged screamer conceived and constructed in the tiny town of Novi, Michigan (the town got its name from the railroad station, which was number six, or No. VI, on the railroad line). The Novis were front-wheel drive cars that put out 550 horses. When they debuted in 1948, Duke Nalon ran off and hid from the field until a bubble in his gas tank caused an extra fuel stop, and he wound up third. He and Rex Mays returned in 1949, and Nalon captured the pole. But Nalon walked away from a terrifying crash, and many drivers became spooked by the big V-8s. In later years, the great Jim Hurtubise qualified a Novi second and led the first lap of the 1963 500-mile race.

Most other cars—even thundering NASCAR coupes and California hot rods with bodies made from aircraft fuel tanks—were becoming easier to drive. Much of the better handling could be attributed to tires rather than sophisticated suspensions, though American automobile engineers began to make great strides once allowed to work on new chassis designs in the late 1940s. Power steering and power brakes prevented muscle strain, and the automatic transmission, first offered as Hydra-matic in a six-cylinder 1938 Oldsmobile, made smooth getaways a sure thing. For those who could not get used to the idea of a floorboard without a clutch, Chrysler offered models into the 1950s that blended automatic shifting with a third pedal!

On the Grow in Kenosha

In 1946, two years before the first rod and custom car show in Los Angeles and the year of the first drive-up bank in Chicago, a sizeable addition to Snap-on's Kenosha facility was constructed. This undertaking provided for an entirely new area for automatic machinery, plus increased steel storage, and a larger die sinking department. Originally, Snap-on was well on the outskirts of the city, which grew haphazardly toward and then around it. For some strange reason, people built their dream homes within 100 yards of Snap-on's forge shop, then later complained about the noise. Today, the plant juts out of a pleasant residential neighborhood.

This 1954 Nash Metropolitan proved that American Motors, with George Romney as its president, was interested in building smaller cars.

Further additions were made in 1953 and 1959, bringing the Kenosha plant to 162,000 square feet. To the north,

Snap-on completed a manufacturing and administration facility in Long Branch, Ontario, in 1952. Herramientas Snap-on de Mexico, also a subsidiary, made its first sale in 1952. The Mt. Carmel, Illinois, plant added a modern forge shop and other production areas in 1955. Obviously, demand for Snap-on products was strong and growing.

Because so much technology was poured into the war effort, automotive progress stood still—except in one area. B.F. Goodrich of Akron, Ohio, engineered a synthetic-rubber tire in

1940. Made of butadiene, which had been synthesized from air, natural gas, petroleum, and soap, the tires were trademarked Ameripol. Seven years later, the same company brought out the first tubeless tires. These tires automatically sealed themselves when punctured, a feat anyone who has ever had a blowout can appreciate. After being marketed in Indiana, Kentucky, Ohio, and West Virginia, they were sold nationwide.

New-car models showed up again in 1946, but they were essentially prewar designs. Postwar designs were eagerly awaited. The newly designed 1949 Ford, created by industrial designer George W. Walker, was such a hit that sales nearly doubled over the previous year. There was only one problem—Walker had given virtually the same design, five years earlier, to Nash. Walker assumed Nash wasn't going to build his compact car, so he elongated it and sold it to Ford. Nash was forced to change the front end of its vehicle before introducing the entirely new Rambler in 1950. By the time Nash and Hudson merged to form American Motors Corporation in 1954, things were picking up. AMC, Snap-on's longtime Kenosha neighbor and friend, sold 374,240 cars in 1959, the largest number of any independent carmaker to that time.

Chrysler Corporation was the last automaker to offer really fresh, post-World War II designs, and sales suffered because of it. Plymouth lost third place, behind Chevy and Ford, to Buick. Ford continued to narrow the gap with Chevrolet through 1954. Although both Chevrolet and Ford offered an automatic transmission, performance-minded buyers preferred the Ford V-8 over the Chevy straight six. Pontiac, with its L-head straight eight, beat out Plymouth for fourth place in 1954. Some Mercury and Lincoln models were virtually indistinguishable, with the most interesting option being the 1953 Mercury Sun Valley's nicely done tinted-plexiglass partial roof. Cadillac sales hit a record for the make in 1954, reaching 165,959.

Nowadays, the Fifties seem like an idyllic time in American life—cars were cheap and became much more interesting as the decade progressed. Many things were afoot during the period, including a $2.8 million Brink's, Inc., armed robbery in Boston and the invasion of South Korea in 1950. The following year, transcontinental television broadcasts began, and J.D. Salinger published *Catcher in the Rye*. President Harry S. Truman seized the steel mills in 1952, his final year in office, to avert a strike. The year 1955 saw more neat cars introduced than at any time within modern memory: Chevrolet finally offered its first V-8 engine, which had overhead valves and 265 cubic inches of displacement, Raymond Loewy created a dazzling shape for Studebakers, and Plymouth attracted widespread attention with "flite sweep" styling.

The same year the first transatlantic telephone cable was laid, 1956, cars got even better looking. Fords were neat in '55 but downright irresistible the next year. With the 1957 Chevy, Ford, and Plymouth models looking sharper than ever, there was hardly time to read Jack Kerouac's new book, *On the Road*, even if it happened to be about riding and driving. By the way, a 1957 Ford Fairlane "500" hardtop sold for $2,800. Detroit stylists must have been carried away with their successes; the 1958 models struggled under pounds of chrome and growing fins to look mediocre. Were they distracted by Sputnik late in '57, or America's Explorer I satellite response early in '58? Regardless, Detroit products proved visually disappointing for the rest of the decade, though with the admission of Alaska and Hawaii as states in 1959, there was at least one more long driving vacation to take.

Detroit's Thundering V-8s

Technical matters made great strides in the 1950s. Unusually large, high-compression V-8s, became commonplace. Horsepower (figured very, very optimistically) sold cars and therefore was advertised, never more blatantly than Chrysler in 1956. Chrysler began offering high-performance "hemi" V-8s in 1951, and by 1955 was selling a "300" model, the number based solely on the total of horses produced by a V-8 that had posted a number of stock-car wins in racing form. Cars boasted not just eight cylinders but "Firedome V-8s" and other breathtaking names. Carburetors seemed to grow larger and more numerous with each model change, which had become a sizeable annual event. The only safety feature in an age before seat-belt use was unitary body construction. The construction technique eventually replaced separate chassis and bodies.

Assembling Fords in Dearborn, Michigan, 1953.

Three acquisitions and two retirements marked the decade for Snap-on. Joseph P. Weidenhoff Company in Algona, Iowa, a manufacturer of electronic engine-testing equipment, was purchased in 1956. By 1959, the size of the Algona plant had more than doubled to allow Snap-on to manufacture its own quality tool chests, rollcabs, and cabinets, which previously had been purchased outside. That same year, Snap-on bought the Judson Engineering Company, in Natick, Massachusetts, makers of aligning and wheel-balancing equipment. And in 1960, H.R. Kelsey Welding and Engineering Corporation of Kenosha, which specialized in welding for industry and distribution of welding equipment and gases, became a subsidiary, too.

Bill Seidemann retired in 1954 after thirty-four years with his company, having kept up with field demand for an incredible proliferation of tools and other products. Fellow founder Joseph Johnson handed over the reins to Victor M. Cain in April 1959. Joe retired in 1960 as chairman of the board, but remained on the board as an active member for a number of years (Johnson's progeny remained active in the business with son Donald serving for many years as a top executive, and grandson Greg, a company officer today). Another milestone was passed in 1960 as the last independent branch became part of the company with the purchase of the Snap-on office in St. Louis. Branches had evolved, since the advent of the independent salesperson, into sources of training and dealer assistance, especially in matters of collections and customer financing.

The numbers continued their trajectory. The century's midpoint saw Snap-on sales of $12.02 million and profits of $1.05 million. Five years later, sales were $18.8 million, with profits of

The Joseph P. Weidenhoff Company of Algona, Iowa, a small but respected maker of timing and analysis equipment and other products, was purchased by Snap-on in 1956. This photo, taken in 1967, shows the original facilities and a major addition.

$2.97 million. By 1960 the numbers were $28.32 million and $3.95 million, respectively. Because of the initiative of the newly independent dealers, employment went up only about 25 percent, from 1,850 to 2,500 between 1950 and 1960. Though aided by the return to a free-market economy after the Korean conflict and

an unashamed boom year in 1955, the numbers also resulted from more than 4,000 quality products.

Among the many exciting items in the Snap-on line was the Anal-O-Scope, introduced in 1957. This piece of electronic equipment performed eleven different functions, including those normally done with an engine analyzer and an oscilloscope. The unit checked cams, valves, and more. Other neat stuff offered by Snap-on in the 1950s included a new line of industrial wrenches and hand tools (1950), a timing light and stud removers and resetters

(all in 1952), plus electric impact wrenches (1953). And because consumer awareness of these professional products was growing, the company created its first direct-mail catalogue in 1956. Upscale shade-tree mechanics were shown a chest with "232 time-saving tools in your own rolling workshop," as well as many more modest items.

Who were these weekend mechanics with professional tools in their hands? Though overwhelmingly male, no two were alike. They could be broken down roughly into the following categories:

• Classic/antique car owners and restorers. These guys, from all economic walks of life, tended to be mature and had a real appreciation for the mechanical past. Their heritage was a small group of people who remembered to save classic cars from extinction during the depression days of the 1930s. The '50s owner-restorer spent weekends poking through old barns and junkyards in order to find the correct fender for a Whippet or some other rolling hunk of metallic American history. If home garages expanded during the decade, these fellows must share the blame. But such folks were a good-natured lot, willing to run their restored iron in the local July 4 parade or show it off at the country fair.

• Hot rodders. Young and speedy, these car buffs seemed to spend equal amounts of time performing engine work and at the wheel, profiling at the local drive-in restaurant. Though their initial Snap-on investment may have been modest, they became loyal to the best brands of equipment, without regard to cost. Cars owned by high school kids and those in their early twenties did not have to be new but, first and foremost, they required a dual, nonrestricting exhaust system. They also had to be lowered, with fender skirts, continental kits (an encased, outboard spare tire in the rear), manual transmissions, perhaps dual quads (two four-barrel carburetors), a suicide or necker's knob on the steering wheel, and a V-8 engine—and only a V-8 engine—under the hood.

Founder Joe Johnson in 1959 as he neared retirement after twenty years as president.

Left, This 1952 van was state of the art. The photo is important because vans such as this, run by independent Snap-on salespeople, took to the roads in greatly increased numbers beginning in 1946.

Below, imported cars such as this early 1950s MG TF started the sports car craze in America and opened the doors for other imports. *Courtesy Road America*

• Sports/foreign car owners. Somewhere between the hot rod set and the classic-car clique in age, these folks were stylish, driving Jaguar XK-120s, high-fendered MGs, zippy Triumphs, rear-engine Porsches, and classy Mercedes. They sometimes put up with drafty interiors, alleged heaters, and cartlike suspension systems in order to motor around corners faster than anyone had a right. Let the hot rodders smoke us on the straightaways, they said, we'll catch 'em in the turns. Weekends found sports car owners rallying, holding hillclimbs, racing on parking lots, and working on their machines.

There were variations on all these themes. Farmers or firefighters or even, for sure, mechanics, often performed their own passenger-car maintenance or went racing at the local track or

A load of tools departs Kenosha during the 1950s in an International semi-trailer truck. Post-World War II demand for Snap-on products made many craftspeople, truck drivers, clerical personnel, and others wonderful livings in Snap-on towns.

strip. The car may have been a midget, a sprint car, a modified, a dragster, or a battered sedan, but race these guys did. They certainly required tools, as did fathers and sons tinkering and driving that buzzy little late-1950s inventions, the go-kart. Any or all of these people might be the one person in every neighborhood who

either fixed cars most evenings or would at least tell you what was wrong with yours and about how much it would take to have it made right. With the population at 165 million in 1955 and growing, what an audience!

American Sports Car

General Motors' Chevrolet Division figured in 1953 there was room for an American sports car and brought out the Corvette. The laminated fiberglass body wasn't perfect, the car had only a six-cylinder engine, and a Powerglide automatic transmission was standard equipment. Besides, it cost the outrageous sum of $3,250, and all you got for your money was a car thirty-three inches high. Chevy fans hung around, however, voicing encouragement when their favorite brand began producing the V-8 in 1955 and buying in encouraging numbers in 1957 when the Corvette was available with a four-speed transmission and fuel injection. The Corvette, in its forty-second year of production for 1995, bridged the hot rod-sports car gap and, next to Harley-Davidson, may have the most faithful following on the planet.

Ford was at work on a sports car when the Corvette was introduced. Two years later, the 1955 Thunderbird, a two-seater with razor-edge styling, was introduced. Handsome in a different way than the Corvette, the popular T-Bird remained a two-passenger machine for just two years before disappointing sports car buffs by adding a back seat. Today's Thunderbird is a sleek coupe that is the basis of Ford's NASCAR racing program.

Among those who noticed the large, well-to-do, mobile crowd in their Corvettes and Thunderbirds were owners of America's radio stations. Radio, the country's entertainment medium until after World War II, had been eclipsed by television. But TV couldn't travel along with a guy, a girl, and his new convertible. Radio could. The restorer may have listened to country music and the sports car driver to jazz. But rock and roll overpowered the air waves, becoming as indispensable to hot rodders and hot-rod wannabe's as dual exhausts. Rock music ran roughshod across the dial beginning in the mid-'50s. If you doubted that cars and rock went together, you never saw photos of Elvis taking delivery of a new Cadillac.

Not all the good music came from The King. As far back as 1952, Bill Haley sang "Rock-a-Beatin' Boogie." A disc jockey on radio station WJW in Cleveland named Alan Freed heard Haley and coined a phrase from Haley's lyrics that came out "rock 'n' roll." Haley's other hits included "Rock Around the Clock," the theme from a 1955 movie called *Blackboard Jungle*, followed quickly by "See You Later Alligator" and other tunes. No matter where in North America you turned on the car radio, there was Screamin' Jay Hawkins with "I Put a Spell on You," Jan and Arnie singing "Jennie Lee," or Dale Hawkins with "Suzy Q." Speakers

in doors, in dashes, or in back windows quickly proved that cars were great capsules for hearing music.

For mechanics, who may or may not have tuned in as they worked, there weren't enough hours in the day. A 1955 *Wall Street Journal* story estimated that the auto-repair business was a $7 billion market. There were 45,000 new-car dealers, 78,000 independent garages, and 201,000 service stations, and all told they could not keep up with the avalanche of work. Litsinger Ford Co., Chicago, employed sixty mechanics in a 90,000-square-foot facility, fixing more than 100 cars and trucks a day. Still, demand for their expertise exceeded supply. How come? An independent garage owner viewed the repair scene this way: "When they take a V-8 engine and start hanging air conditioners, power steering, power brakes and other gadgets on it, it soon becomes a major operation just to clean the spark plugs. Sometimes we can't even see the part we want to work on."

As registrations climbed, the number of auto shops actually declined. There were 39 percent fewer new-car dealerships, 16 percent fewer service stations, and 1 percent fewer independent shops in 1955 than in 1939. Some 770,000 mechanics and 230,000 apprentices were working themselves into a frenzy. Wichita's vocational high school in 1955 turned out nine auto-mechanic graduates. They received seventy-four job offers! Automakers saw the problem firsthand: General Motors for the 1955–56 model year gave 250,000 mechanics a total of 2.75 million hours of instruction in repairing various parts of GM cars.

Mechanics in the News

Mechanics have always seemed less important to the public than racing drivers, but anyone who followed the Indianapolis 500 heard of A.J. Watson in the late 1950s. A.J. put together the last great generation of front-engine roadsters. With a Watson creation, Rodger Ward in 1959 became the first man to take home $100,000 in a single race when he won the Indy 500 at a speed of 135.9, miles per hour. Ward won with essentially the same car in 1962. Watson was so thorough and Parnelli Jones was so fast that the Californian was able to win in a front-engine Watson machine in 1963, even though rear-engine cars were

continued on page 107

How Nifty Were the Fifties?

Seeing a 1955-1957 Chevrolet, Ford, or Plymouth today makes you want to crawl in the back seat and cuddle past curfew. Detroit products, with their tire-scorching power, accurately represent the fifties, when the people who run things today were kids. Detroit was building cool cars with padded dashboards, wraparound windshields, and lotsa chrome. Almost 58 million cars were manufactured during the 1950s, and the 7.9 million vehicles sold in 1955 would not be exceeded until well into the 1960s.

If cars were in demand, so were houses. When GIs returned to the U.S. in the mid-1940s, they wanted decent places to live. Their prayers were answered by people like William J. Levitt, the first person to offer inexpensive, assembly-line housing. Levitt's Levittowns—hundreds of very similar houses crowded into an instant suburb—sprang up on the East Coast and were imitated everywhere. Families could have modern appliances, individual bedrooms, garages, and lawns for as little as $6,000. Veterans could use low-interest loans to aid them in their big purchase, and builders and developers stayed busy, particularly in large areas outside cities where "plats" were quickly constructed.

Highway construction and the overpowering urges to own cars and homes caused huge social changes. Americans needed cars and decent roads to reach suburban dwellings and to commute from those dwellings back into the central city where most of the jobs remained. With such a major, nationwide expansion under way, jobs were never more important. The quality and quantity of work that paid well were amazing.

Stan's, an early California drive-in restaurant, is seen here around 1950. Good food and comely carhops made this eatery a success. Martin Cable

Unions secured enough money for skilled workers to make them middle class, and huge corporations were paying their white-collar accountants, salespeople, and managers very well.

Young executives operated under rules that often were unwritten but quite rigid. They were expected to socialize after work as part of their jobs, to consume liquor without visible effect, to dress almost as well as their supervisors, to entertain when required, to join country clubs and at least attempt to play golf, and to have a doting and supportive family awaiting them when they returned to suburbia each evening. In return for obedience to the corporation, families enjoyed club memberships, baseball games, and picnics. The income from white-collar jobs purchased washers, dryers, freezers, bicycles, and new cars, and allowed middle-class families to set money aside for their children's higher education. The mood was optimism.

Pressure to buy, buy, buy came from several directions. "Keeping up with the Joneses" meant planned obsolescence—frequently trading cars, purchasing larger television sets, and being as fashionable as the neighbors. Clues to what the neighbors would buy next were found on television, on radio, on the explosion of roadside billboards, and in magazines. Agencies created advertising that came at the consumer in subtle and clever ways. Ads accompanying television shows, for examples, were attuned to the audience. "Dragnet," a tough-talking cop show, was sponsored by Chesterfield unfiltered cigarettes, favored by men. Comedian Milton Berle, with his general audience, was sponsored by Texaco; gasoline was needed by all adult drivers.

The quality of advertising—scripts, visuals, the ability to reach the intended audience—was wonderful, regardless of whether it was of benefit. The Marlboro Man, a handsome, leathery cowboy, silently showed that men smoked and that rugged men smoked Marlboro cigarettes. The cowboy's chiseled features gazed down on commuter traffic from billboards, shown forth at the half of televised football games, and popped up in the

center of news magazines. And a silly little imported car called a Volkswagen, designed before World War II as a cheap form of transportation for residents of Hitler's Germany, used whimsical advertising to reach 200,000 American buyers in 1957 who were more interested in good gas mileage than in tail fins and plush comfort.

The five-day, forty-hour week became standard, leaving middle-class Americans with time on their hands. Some was spent on do-it-yourself projects. Every home sprouted hand tools, power tools, power lawnmowers, hoses and sprinklers, car waxes and shampoos, rakes, hoes, and shovels. Much of the equipment seen stacking up in garages or in lawn sheds was purchased on credit as America discovered plastic. Diner's Club was the first to offer a credit-card method of payment in 1950. It was joined by American Express, then by cards from major oil companies, then by Sears, Roebuck and Co., and others. Consumer debt climbed in the ten years from $73 billion to $196 billion.

After a Saturday of working around the house, the middle class relaxed. Folks grilled burgers, hot dogs, and steaks outdoors, they drank cocktails, beer, and soft drinks (but not much wine), they watched the children wiggle around the neighborhood inside glowing plastic Hula Hoops, and they entertained friends and neighbors. They played recordings of Frank Sinatra or Patty Page on their new stereo phonographs, or they watched "The Life of Riley" on television. Children listened to forty-five rpm rock 'n' roll records on scratchy little portable players, appreciating everyone from Chuck Berry and Fats Domino to Pat Boone and Jerry Lee Lewis. Life was good.

Suburbanites were Republicans, primarily because many had grown up admiring Dwight Eisenhower, the president from 1952 to 1960. Ike helped win World War II, he was the kind of guy it was hard to stay mad at, he presided over the end of the Korean War, and, except for several recessions, was steering the country on an upward spiral. Many sons and daughters of those who had backed Franklin D. Roosevelt and the New Deal voted for Ike—and for his vice president, Richard M. Nixon—in 1952 and 1956.

Harley Earle, General Motors styling chief, at the wheel of the 1951 Buick LeSabre dream car. This particular idea car shows finnage that would adorn Detroit products a few years later. *Used with permission, General Motors Media Archives*

continued from 103

gaining the upper hand. Were mechanics achieving some recognition at last?

They certainly were in the Southeast, as people like Smokey Yunick, Junior Johnson, Holman and Moody, Junie Donlavey, and others worked alongside Chrysler, Ford, and General Motors engineers to make stock-car racing the most competitive form of motor sport anywhere. Like Indianapolis, NASCAR had a large number of wonderful wheelmen in the 1960s—Fred Lorenzen, Lee Petty, son Richard Petty, Fireball Roberts, Curtis Turner, Cale Yarborough, and more. The mechanics squeezed all the juice out of the cars they could, then the drivers would go out onto increasingly big and roomy paved tracks at Daytona or Charlotte and pull each other around the track, nose-to-tail, in the force of their drafts. It was something to see and hear.

Throughout the 1950s, Snap-on kept its fifty-eight branches and hundreds of dealers informed not only about the product but the people who used it. Company publications told of Neville Reiners, chief wrench for Freddy Agabashian's Indianapolis 500 pole-position winning Cummins Diesel Special in 1952. Reiners won numerous Snap-on tools for his expertise. They reported that Don Diedrickson was awarded a Snap-on tool chest in 1956 at the Mountain State stock car races in Helena, Montana. And they pointed out that a prize on the television quiz show, "The Price is Right," was a Snap-on chest taken happily home by Elmer McCord of Grand Prairie, Texas. The brand was making a name for itself.

No one doubted the effectiveness of advertising and promotion. Henry Ford II dismissed the Volkswagen as having no future, then watched clever advertising and a sound, if unexciting, design make the VW the most popular vehicle of all time. Introduced in the mid-fifties, the Beetle was responsible for 4 percent of all cars sold in Amer-

Next page, the 1955 Studebaker President four-door looked clunky and was restyled the following year. For several years in the 1950s, Raymond Loewy created low-slung, memorable Studebakers. Nevertheless, production ceased in the U.S. in 1964 and in Canada in 1966.

Production of tools in Kenosha, 1956. Snap-on enjoyed a number of meteoric years following World War II, necessitating a 27,000-square-foot Kenosha addition in 1953.

ica in 1958. It became a favorite of high school and college kids, and the things done to VWs on the West Coast, from stinger exhausts to wide-track tires and awesome paint jobs, had to be seen to be believed. VW sales were so great that the German automaker assembled cars briefly in Pennsylvania. The last new Beetle in the U.S. was sold in 1976.

The Interstate Highway System

Several events took place in the 1950s that would change forever the look and feel of the United States. Among the most important was passage of the federal Interstate Highway Act of 1956. The bill provided for the construction of 41,000 miles of freeways, to be built over a ten-year period at a cost of $26 billion. The act represented the largest public-works project undertaken in world history. As it turned out, interstate highway construction lasted more than twenty-five years and cost more than $100 billion. But the web of wonderful, multilane roads from one major city to another became a necessity, due in part to the huge numbers of cars being sold.

The I-system was created by a Texan named Francis Turner who grew to manhood as the automobile was coming of age. He could recall Texans working off part of their poll tax by putting in a day's work on local roads. Turner tuned up for the interstate project by planning highways for truck convoys in Alaska during

The 1958 Edsel Ranger. Produced from 1958 to 1960, the Edsel cost Ford as much as $350 million. Despite offering automatic transmission buttons in the center of the steering wheel, the cars were considered ugly and did not sell.

World War II and rebuilding the road system of the Philippines in the late 1940s. His work brought eventual prosperity to the Sun Belt as it succeeded at emptying cities quickly and causing suburbs to sprout. But because some interstate highways ripped through traditional neighborhoods, they were reconsidered. Consequently, the beltways around several cities reminded travelers of doughnuts—good stuff in the circle with a hole in the middle.

And while interstate highways could speed produce to market and goods to outlying areas, they also could spell trouble. Sociologists soon discovered that the broad ribbons of concrete might aid criminals, who could commit a series of felonies in widely separated locales and be well out of the area. Detroit responded by offering law enforcement communications equip-

ment and more exciting, high-speed cars that could run down even the most eager crook's escape. A stock Chrysler 300C was clocked at 176.6 miles per hour in 1960, more than enough speed to overtake even the fastest felon.

Despite the increasing number of on- and off-ramps and other safety features such as wide medians and a white line along the right-hand side of the road, highway deaths nationwide continued to climb. Throughout the fifties, there were 5 million accidents, 40,000 fatalities, and 100,000 permanent disabilities each year. It was of little consolation that better highways were making the number of crashes *per mile driven* decline. As more and more goods moved by truck, the number of car-truck mishaps increased, usually with grisly results to the drivers of cars. All the while, leaded gasoline pumped pollution into the air that was as potentially deadly as it was invisible. Clearly, amid the wonderful cars and wonderful roads, there were problems to be addressed.

#

FROM DRIVE-INS TO DRIVING SMARTER, 1960-1980

The sixties were restless times, to say the least. African Americans and others sat in for equal rights, numbering 70,000 participants in the first eight months of 1960. The following year, Alan B. Shepard, Jr., rocketed into suborbital space flight in a Mercury capsule, and the year after that Rachel Carson's book *Silent Spring* helped launch the modern environmental movement. A nuclear test-ban treaty was inked in 1963, followed in 1964 by omnibus civil-rights legislation. Most of the U.S. northeast and parts of two Canadian provinces suffered a massive electric power blackout in 1965. In 1966, Medicare began paying for a portion of the health care of Americans over the age of sixty-five. Rioting ripped inner cities, including Detroit, in 1967, and in 1968 North

The 1968 Camaro Sport Coupe. Its attractive styling has challenged the Ford Mustang and other pony cars since its introduction in 1967.

The revolutionary "Flank Drive" wrench design was patented in 1965.

An A&W Drive-In, circa 1960. Roy Allen bought a root beer formula from a chemist and opened the first drive-in restaurant on the West Coast in Sacramento in 1921. Tray boys served customers, and the franchise grew. *A&W Restaurants, Inc.*

Snap-on Everywhere

Big things were afoot at Snap-on during the decade. By 1960, there were branches all over the place—there was even a Koreans captured the *U.S.S. Pueblo*. Woodstock drew nearly half a million members of the counterculture to a soggy weekend of music in upstate New York in 1969.

Snap-on dealer in Beirut! In 1964, the company acquired its first IBM computer. The system replaced punch-card equipment and improved order processing and replenishing inventory. South of the border, Snap-on added production facilities in Mexico, where a distribution system was already in place. Direct sales began the following year in the United Kingdom, a step in transplanting Snap-on marketing methods to Europe. The company's Canadian subsidiary, which expanded greatly during the decade, supplied many of the products for this potentially vast market.

The first Mustang was unveiled in the fall of 1963 for the 1964 model year. Offered as a two-door, the car did wonders for the company's image with baby boomers, the first wave of which turned sixteen the same year the Mustang was intro-

People changed, too. Victor M. Cain became chairman of the board and chief executive officer, while Robert L. Grover was elected president. One other fellow, Rod Palmer, retired in 1967. The senior vice president was the son of Stanton Palmer, and he spent his entire working life at the company in which his father had seen such potential. At the same time, the Snap-on plant in Natick,

Massachusetts, began making its first line of pneumatic tools. The company was poised on the edge of a growth cycle even the most conservative businessperson would call mind boggling.

What was causing such optimism? Among other things, the automobile business was becoming increasingly busy and diverse. America's largest new-car dealer in 1961, "Z" Frank Chevrolet in Chicago, used Snap-on tools extensively, relying on the company's pinpoint diagnostic equipment to realize high productivity in the north-side dealer's fast service facility. That same year, compact cars and vans, such as the Plymouth Valiant

A youthful Mario Andretti recorded seven wins on pavement in capturing the United States Auto Club national championship in 1966. He also qualified on the pole at Indianapolis in his rear-engine Ford.

and the Ford Econoline, began showing up in large numbers. By the last week of March 1963, Snap-on was realizing $1 million a week in sales. To reach younger, less affluent mechanics and car buffs, the company introduced the less expensive Par-X line of tools. This was, after all, a golden age for shade-tree mechanics.

It was an exciting time at the races, too. The last event on the beach at Daytona occurred in 1958, with the gigantic Daytona International Speedway opening the following year. Two

This is the convertible model of the 1968 Chevrolet Camaro, one of the prettiest muscle cars ever to hit the street. Created to combat Ford Mustang sales, Camaros remain in production to this day, favorites of the young and the speedy. *Used with permission, General Motors Media Archives*

years after that, in 1961, The Firecracker 250 at Daytona became the first NASCAR Grand National event to be shown on network television. It appeared on ABC's "Wide World of Sports." Competition was intense as drivers from increasingly diverse backgrounds signed on to run the stock-car circuit. Fred Lorenzen, a Chicago-area native, became the first Grand National driver to win more than $100,000 in a single season when he took home $113,750 in 1963. Later in the decade, Indy drivers such as A.J. Foyt and Mario Andretti would be lured south to compete with Buddy Baker, David Pearson, Richard Petty, and others.

Drag racing also attracted attention. NHRA, the National Hot Rod Association, was a spawn of the Southern California Timing Association, a bunch of guys who stripped cars of their bodies to create quarter-mile "rail jobs." In their search for power, the drag racers got to fooling with nitromethane, a skittish, dangerous fuel that was outlawed from 1957 to 1964. Sanctioning by the NHRA tended to legitimize drag racing, which began attracting major auto-oriented sponsors later in the 1960s. At the end of the decade, there were dozens of great strips all across the country with names like Englishtown and Pomona and Indianapolis Raceway Park.

The Consumer Crusader

Yet beneath the surface, the automotive industry had some problems. They were personified by a dark-haired, intense young man by the name of Ralph Nader. An attorney, Nader possessed neither a car nor a driver's license, yet he would have far-reaching effects on the business. Rumors had circulated for several years about General Motors' Chevrolet Corvair, a rear-engine, rear-drive compact. The rumors indicated that the car, driven at excessive speeds in untrained hands, could act unpredictably. Nader published *Unsafe at Any Speed* in 1964, which he claimed confirmed these and other rumors. He used money from the sale of the book to persuade Congress that automobile safety was being neglected.

There was just enough truth in Nader's allegations that both politicians and the public took notice. He pointed out that Detroit should spend as much money on the safety of each car as on the way it looked—some $700 was used in styling every Big Three product. He insisted on seatbelts, better bumpers, stronger protection in case of a rollover, and more. General Motors tried to entrap Nader, and the company was forced to apologize before a Senate committee. The "Consumer Crusader" won almost $500,000 in damages from them, which he spent to apply more pressure to automakers. Two results were the Highway Safety Act and the Traffic Safety Act, signed into law on September 9, 1966, three years before the Corvair went out of production. Automotive people were insulted by the politicians, who preferred to believe a nontechnical amateur.

All the while, Snap-on worked to improve its products. In 1965, for example, the U.S. Navy began to experience problems in removing small, twelve-point fasteners from their aircraft. The corners of the fasteners would round off under high torque conditions using conventional wrenches. Snap-on developed the revolutionary "Flank Drive" design, wherein the socket made contact with the nut or bolt away from the

Chevrolet Corvettes were restyled for 1968, showing the so-called Coke-bottle shape. Constant attention to refinement of the fiberglass body, power, and handling resulted in a big and powerful two-seater with a huge following. Displacement from its V-8 engine has ranged as high as 454 cubic inches over the years. *Used with permission, General Motors Media Archives*

corner for better turning and more widely distributed stress. Several years of legal debate resulted in Flank Drive receiving a patent. Offered initially on special, high-performance tools, Flank Drive was later adopted on most company wrenches and sockets. As patents expired, the better competitors came out with their own versions—sincere forms of flattery.

Gene Olson, Snap-on's chief engineer, recalls that the military approached Snap-on for help following the Korean War. U.S. fighter jets were creating so much heat and vibration that fasteners required huge amounts of torque to turn them. Besides solving the problem with Flank Drive, Snap-on and the Amerace Corporation won a contest to design a combination tool and fastener for aerospace use. The winning entry, made up of radial splines, was sold to General Electric and became a military standard. Today, every commercial and military jet aircraft is held together with spline fasteners. "They were of even more benefit than flank drive, because they were something entirely new," Olson notes.

No one was using tools with more flourish at this time than the West Coast's fabricators of hot-rod cars. Names like George Barris, Dean Jeffries, and Ed "Big Daddy" Roth brought fresh perspectives to customizing automobiles. They did not feel constrained by any given model's original shape; instead, they chopped, channeled, chiseled, shortened, widened, or lowered staid old cars to give them a look the designers never intended. Powered by huge V-8s, frequently with superchargers or fuel injection, the cars were seen in dozens of new hot-rod magazines and in a series of mindless beach movies that somehow connected cars, surfing, girls, and second-rate surf music. Nevertheless, a machine painted by Von Dutch or some other vehicular

Bevo Boats and Weinermobiles

Automobiles caught the public's eye from the start. Within a few years, after cars had become so common they no longer attracted a crowd, businesses kicked their mobility into a higher gear, creating the promocar. Two wonderful examples are Anheuser-Busch Bevo Boats and Oscar Mayer Weinermobiles.

St. Louis-based Anheuser-Busch (A-B) saw Prohibition coming as early as 1916. Consequently, the company began to extol the benefits of its brewer's yeast and to export more and more Budweiser. It also introduced a new beverage that tasted like beer without the alcohol, naming it Bevo. A mix of barley malt, rice, hops, yeast, and water, Bevo got its name from "pivo," the Bohemian word for beer. Bevo debuted in 1916, and by 1918, just before nationwide Prohibition began, was selling five million cases per year.

Promotion-minded folks at Anheuser-Busch followed up the introduction of the soft drink by constructing a Bevo Boat—a boatlike body riding on a Pierce-Arrow chassis. The brewer offered it to the U.S. government, which took it on tour in 1917 to help sell war bonds. Several models of the Bevo Boat followed, each more nautical in appearance than the last. Ironically, sales of Anheuser-Busch brewer's yeast helped spell the demise of Bevo. The yeast became so popular for making home-brewed beer that sales of nonalcoholic Bevo withered. The last case shipped, and the final Bevo Boat constructed, occurred in 1929.

The talent that created the Bevo Boat stayed busy throughout the 1920s, building a number of significant vehicles. Refrigerator-truck bodies, armored-car bodies, utility bodies, and more were made by the gang in St. Louis. The A-B vehicle department developed the Lampsteed Kampcar, one of the very first recreational vehicles, complete with beds and cooking equipment, for the Model T chassis. Bus bodies, horse vans, even predecessors of the modern station wagon were turned out by brewers with time on their hands. All such work of course stopped with Prohibition's end, which took place on Dec. 5, 1933.

The 1995 Oscar Mayer Weinermobile. **Courtesy Oscar Mayer**

Care for a hot dog with your beer? The folks at Oscar Mayer, the mammoth maker of meat products in Madison, Wisconsin, to this day run a fleet of Weinermobiles. A dozen fresh-faced college students drive six of the hot dog-and-bun shaped vehicles to various attractions, all summer, all across the country.

The first such vehicle was fabricated from metal by the General Body Co. of Chicago in 1936. The thirteen-foot-long original had two open cockpits. A glass enclosure to protect the driver was added later. Five Weinermobiles were built by Gerstenlager of Wooster, Ohio, in the early '50s, on Dodge chassis. These vehicles had buns for fenders and toured for many years. One is part of the Henry Ford Museum collection at Greenfield Village in Dearborn, Michigan.

Brooks Stevens of Milwaukee designed a futuristic, bubble-nosed Weinermobile in 1958 (when he wasn't designing Excaliburs and other cars). Constructed of fiberglass on a Jeep chassis, this model suffered from mechanical woes and was rebuilt before retiring in the early 1960s. Oscar Mayer mechanics put together two of the vehicles in 1969. One is in service to this day in Puerto Rico. A styrofoam and fiberglass version was built on a motorhome chassis in 1976 and is cookin' along in Spain at the moment.

Brooks Stevens also designed the six contemporary creations. They're a majestic twenty-three feet long, sit on a Chevrolet van chassis, weigh 5,800 pounds and are powered by a Chevy V-6 engine. The twelve college students who drive the vehicles around the U.S. are known collectively as Hot Doggers. They've nicknamed them Weinerbagos, and they advise each other to "watch your buns" when backing or parking. New versions are just now being introduced.

Makes the tidy, white Snap-on van look rather restrained, doesn't it?

Land Cruisers

Three Novelty Automobiles that tour the country in behalf of Anheuser-Busch Products

Budweiser III
Famous new land boat 19 feet long. Mounted on a Pierce-Arrow Chassis. Radio equipped and replete with attractive mountings. Built by Anheuser-Busch, Truck Body Division.

Budweiser II
Designed and built by Anheuser-Busch. This land cruiser is also mounted on a Pierce-Arrow Chassis and is radio equipped. Its brilliant metal mountings and colorful body make it the center of attraction wherever it goes.

Budweiser IV
This beautiful boat on wheels is a sister ship to Budweiser III and shares in the touring of the country with its two mates. It embodies all the appurtenances of Budweiser III and was also built by Anheuser Busch.

Built by the Anheuser-Busch Truck Body Division, this is one of several Bevo Boats fabricated on Pierce-Arrow chassis during Prohibition. Courtesy Anheuser-Busch Archives

No car was more overwhelming in any form of racing than the Can-Am McLarens. The rear-engine, Chevrolet-powered cars dominated Group 7 road racing in the late 1960s. *Courtesy Road America*

artist was sure to draw a crowd.

So were people like Don Garlits. A Floridian, Garlits is a great example of the kinds of folks who made drag racing so successful. After several years of running equipment through the quarter-mile, Garlits broke speeds of 170, 180, then 200 miles per hour with a slingshot dragster he called *The Swamp Rat*. A solid mechanic and designer, Garlits survived several crashes and recovered from burns to win national championships—ahead of many Californians. Kids all over the country saw the Dodge-powered *Wynnscharger* roar down the strip. They did the same thing in

their old car or in Dad's new one. Long before drag racing was regularly televised, Don Garlits, his cars, and other worthy quarter-milers such as Don "The Snake" Prudhomme or Grumpy Jenkins were known to anyone who cared about automobiles.

Those who cared included fans of the Can-Am and Trans-Am, two series that attracted crowds of 50,000 or more to road-racing courses from Lime Rock, Connecticut, to Riverside, California. The Can-Am featured large, single-seat streamlined machines with huge, usually Chevrolet, motors. There were many stars in the series, but no one dominated like Bruce McLaren and Denis Hulme in McLaren cars. They chewed up and spat out virtually every kind of sports car, at one point winning twenty-three races in succession. Drivers like Mark Donohue and Parnelli Jones starred in Trans-Am racing, where muscle cars such as AMXs, Barracudas, Camaros, Mustangs, and Trans Ams challenged Porsches, Nissans, and Audis.

Muscle cars, on which Trans-Am-type machines were based, could trace their lineage back to 1964. That year, Ford introduced the wildly popular Mustang and Pontiac the tire-smoking GTO. Initially, the Lee Iacocca-led team that created the Mustang was looking to make a fun car for young drivers, many of them female. But within a few years Ford was stuffing powerful V-8s into their compact car and squaring off against Camaros and Trans-Ams, which GM built to outmuscle the competition. The cars may have passed the point of credibility at Plymouth and Dodge in the early '70s. Superbirds, sporting cartoon characters on the fenders and rear wings that stuck a couple of feet above the purple or lime or ebony trunk, could be spotted from Woodward Avenue in Detroit to Van Nuys Boulevard in Los Angeles.

Catalogues to Remember

Visually, Snap-on began to acquire a modern look, though more subdued than your average Dodge Hemi 'Cuda. By 1973, the annual tool catalogue, which grew almost geometrically in thickness, assumed its familiar black-and-red color theme and current four-color process. The Snap-on-created book was so thick with products that the index alone took up five pages of small type. The mechanic on the cover had long hair and sideburns, like most everyone else in those days. The company had for several years sold its products based on tool speed, or productivity, and since the mid-1960s had worked closely with automakers to ensure that there were tools available to fix the very latest domestic and foreign models. The Blue Point name was fading, but as late as 1966 it could still be found on items such as valve seat grinder sets.

More important than the way the company appeared was the way it performed. Snap-on sold $50.8 million worth of goods in 1967, realizing nearly $9 million dollars in profit. Sales the following three years were $57.9 million, $66.2 million, and $76.5 million, with profits of $11.5 million, $12.7 million, and $14.9 million respectively. If you were a shareholder, things were great and getting better. By 1972 the company's sales were an awesome $105 million, with profits of $20.7 million—and continuing to rise. The '72 annual report, by the way, noted that 70 percent of sales came from the dealer direct to the customer, proving the wisdom of the Snap-on method of selling.

"The World's Largest Independent Maker and Marketer of Quality Hand Tools and Equipment," read the subhead beneath the logo. Monetary figures continued to make the motto no exaggeration. By 1976, annual sales were $212 million, with $35 million in profit. Incredibly, two short years later saw the figures at $309 million and $64 million, respectively. By 1979, with 3,000 independent dealers working, the company sold $373 million worth of tools and other goods and pocketed $76.5 million for its trouble. Words of caution about the economy from presidents such as Norman E. Lutz (1974–1978) only showed how prosperous the company, its eleven plants, and its products really were, in good times and bad.

Not everyone in Kenosha fared as well as Snap-on. Longtime cross-town friend American Motors, formerly Nash, saw acceptance of its products tail off badly. Only Jeep, acquired in 1970 and assembled in Ohio, remained healthy throughout the period, thanks in part to the installation of an optional V-8 engine in 1965 and, introduction of the luxurious Jeepster in 1971. AMC decided in 1979 to produce French Renaults in its Kenosha factory, thereby keeping its people employed. The company no longer made muscle-type cars such as the late '60s Javelin, nor did it have much to offer of its own except the awkward-looking Pacer. Meanwhile, Snap-on fortunes were literally out of this world.

The end of the 1960s saw Apollo 11 astronauts land on the moon. Snap-on tools were a part of the project, which began for the company with a meeting back in 1964. Snap-on's New Orleans branch, at the request of Boeing, Chrysler, and General Electric, collaborated on a special type of tool that could be used in clean rooms. (A clean room has electronically filtered air containing no more than 100 particles of dust per cubic foot. The average home has one million particles per cubic foot.) Clean rooms are required wherever tiny, vital electrical and mechanical components are assembled. The standard Snap-on tool at the time was plated electrically with nickel and then chrome in a

Roger Penske (right, in yellow sweater) made the AMC AMX a winner in Trans-Am road racing in the late 1960s with Mark Donohue at the wheel. *Courtesy Road America*

dipping process. The inside of the tools, which slid over the dipping rack, was left unplated and later sprayed. That wasn't good enough.

Chrome and aluminum are subject to flaking under some conditions, causing possible contamination. Snap-on tools intended for use in a clean room were vapor honed (a form of sandblasting) to achieve minimum porosity. They were then nickel plated without using electricity in a patented method that coated all surfaces. All tools with handles required an inert DuPont plastic made of Delrin because the substance would not break down in ultrasonic cleaning solutions. Cape Kennedy's clean rooms were outfitted with Snap-on's special tools, the astronauts landed on the moon and, more important, took off, and the Kenosha-based company celebrating its forty-ninth year in 1969 won a small but important new market.

Speaking of markets, way back in 1951 Snap-on foresaw the popularity of foreign cars coming. In an article called "A Market in the Making," the company pointed out to salespeople that it was printing new metric and Whitworth catalogues for the nimble machines imported exclusively from Europe at the time. U.S. Department of Commerce figures show that the first significant year for Japanese car imports began about 1964. That year, 16,023 Japanese vehicles competed for showroom space with 364,683 cars from Germany; 77,548 cars from the United Kingdom; 39,352 from France; 18,562 from Sweden; 10,843 from Italy; and 9,201 from Canada. The 536,325 total accounted for less than 1 percent of total U.S. registrations.

A Japanese Foothold

But while vehicles from other countries would catch on and fade, or sell in only limited numbers, Japanese cars secured a niche in this country and then occupied other slots by introducing new models. German imports peaked in 1971 at 770,807 before falling to less than half that number by 1990. Americans bought 102,344 Italian cars in 1975; 50,032 French cars in 1982; and 106,710 British cars in 1982; today, not many machines from these three countries reach the U.S. Swedish sales peaked

The 1969 Plymouth Barracuda. Another pony or muscle car, the Barracuda was available with an optional hemispherical-head V-8 that produced awesome power at the strip, on a road course, or at a stop light.

at 148,700 in 1986, the same year the first Korean car reached North American shores. Canadian sales in the U.S. exceeded one million units six of the last seven years of the 1980s, due largely to the fact that Chrysler minivans are built in large numbers there.

The Japanese grabbed hold of the American market and simply refused to let go. They started modestly enough on the West Coast with Datsuns (today's Nissan) and Toyotas. The first popular sedans were the Datsun 510 and the Toyota Corona. The former could be crafted into a modest high-performance car while the latter was compact in size but featured a smooth engine and a comforting interior. Several other Japanese makes joined Datsun and Toyota on the West Coast, but none so successfully as Honda. The world's largest motorcycle maker began modestly with a front-drive, crossed-engine subcompact. There followed Honda Civics and Accords, as well as Prelude coupes and more. Japanese automakers eventually would open assembly plants in the U.S., but none would be more successful than Honda.

Although the seventies should have been a period of recuperation, they proved otherwise. Events came thick and fast as millions of Americans in the spring of 1970 staged anti-pollution demonstrations in connection with the first Earth Day. The voting age was lowered to eighteen the following year, and the year after that five men were arrested in the Watergate office complex for having illegally entered Democratic Party headquarters. In 1973, Vice President Spiro T. Agnew resigned and the military draft came to an end. President Richard M. Nixon resigned before he could be impeached in connection with Watergate in 1974, and Gerald R. Ford was sworn in. Patty Hearst was kidnapped in 1975, the year before the nation's Bicentennial. A Cabinet-level Department of Energy was formed in 1978, and in 1979 the federal government underwrote loans totaling $1.5 billion for the foundering Chrysler Corporation.

For either dedicated car enthusiasts or mere operators, the decade's most trying time involved the oil embargo of 1973-74. From October 19, 1973 to March 18, 1974, Arab oil-producing states did not sell a drop of oil to anyone who had supported Israel in the 1973 Arab-Israeli war. That included, of course, the United States. American car owners queued all over the country

The Datsun 240-Z, shown in its 1973 configuration, was at one time the world's most popular sports car. As much as any vehicle, this sharp six-cylinder import made consumers realize that the Japanese were designing and building quality products.

as filling-station owners doled out precious gasoline and prices climbed every few days. Prior to the embargo, gasoline was almost obscenely inexpensive. It had risen from about thirty cents in 1960 to thirty-seven cents ten years later. Before 1973 ended, it hit fifty-four cents a gallon and continued upward. Large cars that turned in poor gas-mileage figures suddenly became known as "stoves" among car salespeople. The vehicles languished in showrooms as buyers purchased smaller, more efficient automobiles.

There was a run on small cars. Those offered by domestic makers—AMC's Gremlin, Ford's Pinto, General Motors' Vega—simply did not compare in quality or features to automobiles coming in from Japan. The Japanese were the big winners of the oil embargo, as people who might not have considered a foreign car earlier found themselves enjoying relative comfort, adequate performance, and mileage they'd never before experienced. When these drivers were ready for larger cars, so were the Japanese. Detroit's answers to Accords and Corollas were cars like the

One year, Ron Thurston was thundering along as part of a truck convoy in Long Binh, South Vietnam. The next, he was rolling down the highway in his new Snap-on van.

"I saved $3,000 in Vietnam," recalls the Sun Prairie, Wisconsin, dealer in his twenty-sixth year with the company as of 1995. "I was able to finance the rest." Financing, via weekly payments, is an important part of Thurston's business. Mechanics of all age ranges and experiences purchase tools from him following their credit approval by Snap-on. The Milwaukee branch, some seventy miles to the east, qualifies customers and Ron does the rest.

"I finance 80 percent of the tools I sell. The average mechanic who's been in business five years may have $10,000-15,000 worth of tools, but he's always adding. Many of the people with big sets still buy something from me every week."

Thurston is one of several Snap-on dealers covering the Madison metropolitan market—an area in south-central Wisconsin with about 300,000 residents. His clients may work for car dealers, for independent garages, for truck dealers, or for contractors. Mechanics who have turned to him as their tool source have even served places such as marinas, airports, and golf courses. The Snap-on dealer who is willing to use his imagination can find a lot of new markets. "I have a Maytag dealer here in town who calls me a couple of times a year," he says.

Because Thurston has stuck with the program,

Ron Thurston has been selling Snap-on tools to folks in and around Sun Prairie, Wisconsin, ever since he saved enough money while in Vietnam to make a down payment on a franchise. Thurston is mechanically inclined— he maintains his own van—and he's a fan of auto racing.

he has a spacious, separate garage and shop where he keeps and maintains his van. The 1984 Chevrolet has 111,000 miles on it. He estimates that he drives about 10,000 miles a year in calling on his customers. He has competitors, but they have neither the name nor the ability to cover the Madison area as regularly and thoroughly as Ron and his fellow Snap-on dealers. "I visit every customer once a week," he notes. "I leave the house between 6:30 and 7 A.M., I'm never more than twenty miles away, and there are no overnights."

The Snap-on guys in the Madison area have a number of customers who work on other people's cars all week long, then work on their own racers each weekend. Consequently, it was natural for the dealers to get involved in racing sponsorship at the one-third mile dirt oval in Sun Prairie, as well as at a couple of other area tracks. Thurston has been a big sprint car, IndyCar, and stock-car fan as long as he can remember.

"The best driver I ever saw run midgets at Sun Prairie? That's a tough one. Stan Fox from Janesville was good, Rich Vogler was good. Jeff Gordon, from Indiana, was as good as any body I've seen. He won the Brickyard 400 in '94 and he's done real well in NASCAR." Obviously, when Thurston and his fellow dealers entertain customers at a Day at the Races, he pays attention. And although he has more years of service than most, Ron is a typically successful independent retailer of Snap-on automotive tools. Not a bad job.

Chevrolet Cavalier, which were imitations but not always good imitations. By 1980, Detroit could claim a monopoly among only two kinds of buyers—young drivers, who wanted a muscular Mustang or Camaro or Trans-Am, and elderly drivers of large cars.

Metrics in Demand

The Japanese invasion, and the later concept of producing and selling a world car here in the U.S., was fortuitous for Snap-on. America's most prestigious tools now were sought after in metric sizes! Dealers found rookie and veteran mechanic alike patronizing them in order to work on a Subaru or a Saab, a Mazda or a Mercedes-Benz. In order to keep pace with overall demand, not just metric, two plants were purchased in Tennessee, a new plant was built in Milwaukee, and a research and development center was established in the Chicago suburb of Bensenville. Becoming a world-class company resulted in $30 million in sales in Great Britain alone in 1980. That was the same figure reported for total corporate net sales in 1962. A West German branch was opened in 1977 to meet demand in central Europe.

Due to the fact that Snap-on was attracting a lot of interest in the financial community, the company was listed on the New York Stock Exchange in 1978. That same year, Edwin C. Schindler was elected president of the corporation. The company's growth was a combination of careful planning and, from the company's point of view, world events that put a positive spin on the business. Part of Snap-on's grass-roots success was a replacement policy put in place early and reinforced in the 1970s: "Any tool found to be defective in material or workmanship will be repaired or replaced." This no-questions-asked approach gives dealers and customers alike a great deal of confidence in the product.

With expansion came an ever increasing number of tools. By the mid-1970s, disc brakes were standard on the front wheels of virtually all cars. These brakes required different tools than traditional drums, as did such items as fuel injection and on-board computers. The company automotive-tool catalogues in 1973 totaled 609,850 copies, weighed 751,435 pounds, required a 300-hour press run, and filled nineteen semi-trailers. After all,

sales exceeded $100 million for the first time in 1972, $200 million for the first time by 1976, and $400 million for the first time by 1980.

Racing on the Grow

The twenty years covered in this chapter saw a revolution in racing. With the able assistance of television and superior color motion-picture film, races run in the afternoon could be moved around by satellite and highlighted on the sports portion of the nightly news that same evening. It didn't take long for breathtaking photo-finishes, nose-to-tail drafting, and spectacular accidents to attract legions of fans and viewers. The Indy 500 suffered a foreign invasion in the early 1960s as names like Jim Clark and Graham Hill advanced the rear-engine revolution. Down south, stock cars became more sophisticated as streamlining subtleties subtracted tenths of seconds from lap records. David Pearson won an incredible sixteen races in 1968, and NASCAR unveiled another superspeedway in Talladega, Alabama, in 1969. By 1970, Buddy Baker was turning 200-mile-per-hour laps in a Dodge.

No one was better at racing during the period than A.J. Foyt. He won his first Indy car title in 1960 after qualifying for his first Indy 500 in 1958. He won the Indianapolis 500 in 1961, the first of an incredible four victories at the track. Foyt took a total of seven Indy car titles, the last in 1979. His career includes forty-one USAC stock-car wins, twenty-nine wins in sprint cars, twenty in midgets, seven in NASCAR stocks, seven in sports cars, and two in championship dirt cars. Foyt also teamed with Dan Gurney to win the 24 Hours of LeMans in a Ford Mark IV in 1967. At one time or another he broke his back, sustained arm injuries, and suffered serious leg and foot injuries. Because he was such a force in racing for so many years, he was named a 1993 Sports Legend by the American Sports Broadcasters Association. Only two others, Muhammad Ali and Arthur Ashe, have been so honored.

Richard Petty was to NASCAR as A.J. Foyt was to Indy Car competition. Petty, the son of a racer, took home his seventh and final NASCAR title in 1979. That same year, CBS-TV broadcast the Daytona 500 in its entirety, and Petty set a single-

Handsome red Snap-on tool boxes await shipping at Algona, Iowa, in 1979.

Right, this is the original Shelby Cobra, an English AC car with a Ford V-8 stuffed under the hood. Cobras competed successfully in U.S. road racing beginning in 1963. *Courtesy Road America*

season record for winnings with a combined purse of $531,292. Like A.J. Foyt, who had a rearview mirror full of young Rick Mears, NASCAR rookie Dale Earnhardt gave Petty and others a great deal to think about. Earnhardt captured $200,000 in prize money in 1979, the initial year of a career that continues its upward spiral to this day and includes seven NASCAR titles. The record books are crowded with great names from the period, including Tom Sneva, Al Unser, and Bobby Unser in Indy Cars and Bobby Allison, Darrell Waltrip, and Cale Yarborough in NASCAR.

The 55 MPH Limit

Perhaps unfortunately, speeds on public roads and high-ways were going down as speeds on strips and tracks were headed upward. Legal maximum speeds on interstate highways in the early 1970s were seventy miles per hour. A federal national limit of fifty-five was put in place in the wake of the oil embargo, and that maximum made wide-open spaces an ordeal to drive across. In fact, more crowded areas of the country such as the Northeast hardly noticed the new limit, whereas folks in Texas or Arizona or Wyoming pointed out that scooting across their

states at a smart pace had always been a part of their lives.

Drivers running at slower speeds had time on their hands, so cars became rolling billboards. A number of states introduced premium-priced license plates so that car owners could express themselves in six to eight letters. DR ZITS was a dermatologist, ACELR8 was a speedy soul, and AMAMOY was meant to be read in a rearview mirror. Bumper stickers proliferated. They covered politics, religion, sports, drivetime radio, views on war and peace, ads for cheap daycare, notices that the driver was the parent of an honor-roll student, and brief statements that weren't always in good taste. Would you more readily avoid a car with a National Rifle Association insignia, or a pink sedan with a Mary Kay Cosmetics sticker? Lower limits gave drivers time to ponder their next traffic move.

It also gave them a time and a place for music on vastly improved, miniaturized sound systems. While those systems could play Vivaldi, Van Morrison, or lessons in French, increasingly they were playing country. Country had a long and honorable history, from the Carter family and Jimmy Rodgers in the 1920s down through Bob Wills and the Texas Playboys, Hank Williams, Ernest Tubb, Roy Acuff, Patsy Cline, George Jones, Buck Owens, and Merle Haggard. New outlaw stars such as Waylon Jennings and Willie Nelson delighted fans in the 1970s. They furnished the atmosphere for car movies such as *Smoky and the Bandit* and TV stuff like "The Dukes of Hazard." Outlaws cut the path for Garth Brooks, Dwight Yoakam, and others.

The line between home and car was further blurred with the introduction of tricked-up vans. Meant originally to transport a horde of hippies or an athletic team, vans took on the look of living rooms, what with velour upholstery, captain's chairs, added glass, small TV sets embedded so that the kids could view cartoons in the back seat, minibars, refrigerators, and more. Years had elapsed since the last custom coachbuilders had executed sweeping automotive designs, but the guys with the greatly improved paint guns were delivering big, square statements that may not have handled well on icy roads but would lug lots of folks and their groceries to a football game or to a family reunion. By the end of the decade, no one thought twice about driving a vehicle with portholes, scallops, and a chrome ladder

They were homely and slow, but every hippie worthy of the label yearned for a Volkswagen Microbus, usually in much worse repair than this model from about 1970.

attached.

The Great Cars

Despite the gas lines and the speed limits, there were a number of great 1970s cars. Among them: Full-sized Ford V-8s, particularly those assembled in Cleveland. They were good looking, and they seemed to run forever. Mazda had produced its millionth rotary engine by 1978, proving that not all Japanese cars were devoid of personality. Buick Rivieras were handsomely restyled in 1974 while the Olds Delta Royale was the company's last convertible for a while and one of its best. Chrysler's best car during the ten-year period was the Cordoba, advertised on television as having "Corinthian leather" seats, among other luxuries. And for those who valued safety and individuality, the Swedes offered roomy Saabs and rock-solid Volvos. Maybe it wasn't such a bad time to be behind the wheel, after all.

THE LOVE AFFAIR FLICKERS AND REKINDLES, 1980-1995

Al Unser, Jr., leads Paul Tracy through the streets of Long Beach in 1994. *George Tiedemann*

The 1980s began momentously as Mt. St. Helens erupted in a blast 500 times more powerful than the first atomic bomb. Recycling became a far-out concept in 1981 as the reusable space shuttle *Columbia* completed a successful mission into space and landing. The following year, 1982, the unemployment rate hit 10.8 percent, the highest since 1940. The Social Security system was saved from bankruptcy in 1983, and in 1984 two American astronauts became the first humans to fly free of a spacecraft. E.F. Hutton had trouble with its checking account in 1985, resulting in a $2 million fine and an $8 million repayment to various banks.

Scandals continued to plague Wall Street in 1986, as Ivan Boesky was fined $100 million, jailed, and barred for life from trading securities. The

Modern Snap-on tool truck. The billboard on the back is from an ad campaign begun in 1994.

first trillion-dollar federal budget was produced in 1987 as the stock market rose phenomenally before crashing in October. The following year, the U.S. suffered through the worst drought in half a century. Employment early in 1989 dropped to 5.3 percent, the lowest total in fifteen years. By mid-1990, the Dow Jones Industrial Average paused at a lofty 2,999.75. A year later, in a cost-cutting move, dozens of military bases were scheduled for closing. All three major U.S. automakers suffered huge losses early in 1992, as did that bulwark of business, IBM, one year later. Happily, in 1994, auto sales were sky-high, new models looked good and ran well, and the economy was sturdy.

Tough Automotive Times

Looking at the 1980s from the start of the decade, things appeared rather dismal. Henry Ford II, who had guided Ford

Motor Company since 1945, saw the future and retired. The grandson of the founder had presided over the debacle of the Edsel and the introduction of the Mustang. Throughout, Ford had maintained market share. But by the first quarter of 1980 the company lost $163.6 million, a drop in the bucket, however, compared to Chrysler's first-quarter loss of $448.8 million. Ironically, while Ford temporarily closed plants and laid off people, Honda announced that it would build a $200 million assembly plant in Marysville, Ohio.

In August 1980, five of every seventeen cars, or 29.3 percent of new-car sales, were foreign. Ford and the United Auto Workers union asked Congress for import limits on the Japanese as the jobless rate refused to dip below 7.8 percent. The severity of the problem was underlined by the third quarter of 1980: Chrysler, Ford, and General Motors all suffered multimillion-dollar losses. Rebates were introduced in an effort to win customers while the duty on small imported trucks, mostly Nissans and Toyotas, was raised. Adding to the woes of the Big Three, their cars weren't breathing easily with the new catalytic converters and additional clean-air devices.

The country paused in 1981 before plunging into a vicious recession. But because every machine from a Chevette to a Ferrari had lots of metric parts, Snap-on did remarkably well. Profits were $68.4 million in 1980, $71.6 million in 1981, and $69.5 million in 1982, the first year in which the corporation attained Fortune 500 status. This was especially heartening in view of the fact that interest rates for things like cars and tools could exceed 20 percent; neither tool buyers nor car buyers wanted to service that kind of debt. Compounding the bad news, gasoline prices soared in 1981 as federal controls were lifted, and highway safety figures indicated that U.S. deaths were on a slight rise, up 1 percent in 1980 to 53,300, despite safer cars.

Snap-on began big-time auto racing involvement late in 1981 when it became associated with four-time Indy 500 winner Rick Mears. Roger Penske's California driver got sales people revved by attending year-end meetings with Snap-on personnel and by serving as the focus of other appearances and advertising efforts. The success of this program led Snap-on's Indianapolis

These and other Snap-on tools were used by astronauts aboard the Space Shuttle in its numerous orbital flights beginning in 1983.

branch in 1984 to open the tool store at the Indianapolis Motor Speedway. This convenience for racing mechanics in turn led the corporation into an association with the Miller Pit Stop competition at the Indy 500 and additional involvement with car owners, their mechanics, and with the sanctioning body.

Oval matters got crazy in 1981, as Bobby Unser won the Indy 500—or did he? Mario Andretti's team claimed that Unser had passed illegally under the yellow caution flag, and Mario

was named the winner until the victory eventually was returned to Unser. At Daytona, Richard Petty took the 500-mile race there in a Buick Regal, one of the new downsized NASCAR vehicles that debuted in 1982. He was followed home by Bobby Allison in a Pontiac LeMans and Ricky Rudd in an Oldsmobile Cutlass. Though downsizing was inaugurated in part to cut speeds and promote safety, King Richard averaged 169.651 miles per hour on his way to victory.

Riding Out the Recession

If 1981 was a dire year domestically, 1982 was when international tool sales suffered. Yet you would never have known it looking at the 1983 Snap-on catalogue, thicker than most phone books at 320 pages and positively oozing color. Edwin C. Schindler served the corporation as president during the tough economic times between 1978 and 1982. He was succeeded by William B. Rayburn from 1982 to 1985. The feds hiked the gasoline tax late in 1982 to cover road repair costs while they also decreed that passive restraint systems (air bags or automatic belts) be installed in 1984 model-year cars. Indy Car racing laid down its own set of regs for the following year, as ground effects

A Childress mechanic tunes Dale Earnhardt's Chevrolet engine using a Snap-on timing light.

were banned in an effort to drop lap speeds on ovals back down to around 220!

The company's most popular racing effort took shape in 1985. "A Day at the Races" was a promotional program that allowed the various branches to bring friends and customers to a variety of racing events. These Snap-on people and end users identified with Rick Mears, who would be named Racer of the Decade, as well as with other drivers. Besides the good will, it further heightened Snap-on visibility and resulted in an increase in tool sales through event-related promotions. Today, branches all across the country entertain about 12,000 customers annually at Indy Car, NASCAR, IHRA, and other automotive events.

Mears may have been the most talented man of the 1980s, but NASCAR driver Bill "Awesome Bill from Dawsonville" Elliott, was the most popular. Snap-on signed on with the stock-car driver in 1985 in order to serve more branches and to reach those fans who believe it's okay for a race car to have fenders! In 1988, Snap-on tools became

Bill Elliot was a NASCAR powerhouse in the mid-1980s. Snap-on signed on to sponsor him in 1985. *George Tiedemann*

Here's a 1986 Taurus, the initial year of production for the popular four-door Ford. The car has been offered with four-, six-, or eight-cylinder engines at one time or another. The curvaceous form, pioneered in the sedan world by Audi, would set the styling tone for Ford cars to the present day. *Courtesy Ford Motor Company*

the Official Tools of CART (now known as IndyCar). The products played a vital role in each entrant's technical inspection by the sanctioning body, and Snap-on was mentioned in trackside announcements, in the souvenir program, and in information handed out to media members covering the event.

A number of non-racing events were making headlines, among them the resurgence of the Chrysler Corporation under Lee Iacocca. The Pennsylvania native stripped the revived number-three automaker to its bones and began to produce better-quality cars with greatly extended warranties in the mid-1980s. He even starred in his own TV ads. Chrysler, Ford, General Motors, and the imports began to offer three-year, 36,000-mile warranties routinely, with even longer warranties on items such as power trains. The automakers in turn demanded quality improvements from suppliers as car manufacturers became assemblers first and foremost. As for Iacocca, he became as well known, and much more respected, than at least one of his former competitors.

John Z. DeLorean did very well for himself in Detroit before deciding in 1973 that he wanted to manufacture and market his dream vehicle. DeLorean chose Ireland as the site of this venture

after receiving a $97 million aid package from the British government. In 1979 he offered the DeLorean, a gull-wing-door sports car with a stainless-steel body, rear engine, and composite chassis. A new government in Britain yanked DeLorean's line of credit after only 5,000 cars were built, and by 1982 the firm apparently was strapped for cash. DeLorean was arrested by FBI agents in Los Angeles with cocaine, evidently enough to underwrite his failing car venture. The automaker was found innocent of trafficking in 1984, despite having said on tape that cocaine was "better than gold."

The car business lost any innocence it might have had in several other ways during the period. Sports-car and Indy Car drivers Don and Bill Whittington and Randy Lanier fled the country after being sought in connection with laundering drug money. John Paul, Jr., a brilliant young Indy Car driver, served time because he was involved in his father's drug business. In fact, Paul Senior shot a man but did not kill him, and Paul Junior got out of jail just in time to run the Indy 500 in 1990! And Tim Richmond, a talented NASCAR driver, died of AIDS in 1989. The thirty-four-year-old Floridian had won seven races in 1988. He battled the disease secretly, once taking his sanctioning body to court after testing positive for two over-the-counter drugs prior to the Daytona 500. Richmond had been the Indy 500 Rookie of the Year in 1980.

Tragedy on the track is part of racing and can be handled better than death elsewhere. Alan Kulwicki, thirty-eight, proved that in 1993 when the newly crowned '92 NASCAR champ died in a private-plane crash during an attempted landing at the airport in Bristol, Tennessee. Kulwicki was a rags-to-riches story, a driven man who spent every dime he had to run and win before he landed major sponsorship. Equally shocking was the death of NASCAR driver Davey Allison, also in 1993. He perished in the wreckage of his helicopter, which he had purchased to move him swiftly from one racing infield to another.

Better Tools for Better Cars

By the time the early 1980s recession ended, Snap-on was deeply involved in computer-assisted tool design. The recently constructed Milwaukee plant, in tandem with research and development operations in Bensenville, Illinois, symbolized the company's commitment to state-of-the-art manufacturing processes. A new branch warehouse/sales office opened in Tampa in 1984, bringing total U.S. branches to fifty-three. A 148,000-square-foot building, purchased in 1983, became the Olive Branch, Mississippi, distribution center. Meanwhile, programs were in place to teach Snap-on's direct-to-mechanic sales approach to its international distributors.

Founder Joseph Johnson died of natural causes in 1986. The immigrant couple's child served for many

This is the latest addition to the Kenosha home office. Snap-on today employs more than 9,000 persons worldwide and has 3,700 dealers and 300 industrial salespersons.

years on the board of directors following his retirement, much of which was spent in Arizona and in northern Wisconsin. Despite his advanced age, his death was a shock to veteran employees and to the Kenosha community. Snap-on marketed 10,000 different items in 1987, and by 1990 there were 5,500 salespersons worldwide. That same year, the corporation became the licensed supplier of tools and equipment for servicing Boeing and McDonnell Douglas aircraft. The start of the 1990s also was a milestone for Snap-on's ratcheting screwdriver—one million had been sold. Neon orange was the most popular handle color for conventional screwdrivers, followed by black, red, yellow, blue, and fluorescent green.

Screwdriver construction changed in 1991, with the implements being case-hardened cryogenically (at low temperatures). The technology involved spraying heat-treated screwdrivers with liquid nitrogen. Sales topped the billion-dollar mark for the first time in 1993, with profits exceeding $85.8 million. A year earlier, Snap-on acquired Sun, the respected maker of diagnostic

What the X-acto knife is to artists the Snap-on Quick Cutter is to auto mechanics. These replaceable-blade knives are designed to give owners a productivity edge.

automotive instruments. As the automobile market matured, the corporation used acquisitions to ensure that its products were available in wider aspects of transportation. Today, Snap-on tools are everywhere, from a Berkeley, California, bicycle shop to a Newport News, Virginia, dry dock, and from a Southeast Asia oil platform to a Canadian auto assembly line.

Diverse industries rely increasingly on industrial products, but the automotive business remains the basis of Snap-on success. The basis for future automotive success, according to the Society of Automotive Engineers, may lie in racing. The SAE recently endorsed racing involvement because the qual-

Next pages, Michael Andretti cuts a corner during an IndyCar race. Michael is one of several sons of drivers who have prospered in competition. *Courtesy Road America*

Dale "The Intimidator" Earnhardt's pit crew springs into action. Earnhardt has won the NASCAR title seven times. The "Goodwrenches" who keep his car running use Snap-on tools.

Left, Chuck Etchells' nitro-burning NHRA Funny Car is Mopar powered and Snap-on wrenched. *Auto Imagery, Inc.*

ity of engineering there is so good. Sanctioning organizations dream up ways to slow the cars, and automobile engineers work within the rules to make them go faster. State-of-the-art tools are needed for such ingenuity. That's why the company today is involved in an array of racing programs:

• Indy Car. In addition to the Indy 500 each May, there is an ongoing commitment to the Championship Association of Mechanics (CAM), the organization representing some 600 IndyCar and Indy Lights mechanics. Several drivers, including the Roger Penske team of Emerson Fittipaldi and Al Unser, Jr., have Snap-on relationships, and the company is heavily involved in the Indy

Grandmother Cleo Chandler is competitive in IHRA events in her Snap-on-backed Chevrolet.

Car race at Long Beach each year. As many as 3,000 guests are hosted by Snap-on, making the event the company's largest Day at the Races. IndyCar events also are strongly supported by Snap-on in Toronto and Vancouver.

- NASCAR. Dale Earnhardt, who notched his seventh NASCAR series championship in 1994, is the son of a race driver who was a dedicated user of Snap-on tools. Consequently, Dale was pleased to associate himself with the company, which is an associate sponsor of the Richard Childress Mr. Goodwrench Chevrolet. Snap-on labeled this contract "our most ambitious step ever in motorsports," and took advantage of Earnhardt's up-front driving and immense following by producing Dale Earnhardt tool-storage units and special tool sets. A number of top NASCAR wrenches use Snap-on tools. As in the Indy Car series, Snap-on was seen on network and cable television throughout the 1994 season.

- IHRA. Young, lean, and exciting, the International Hot Rod Association runs a dozen events from New York to

Right, A typical winged World of Outlaws machine, this one with Stevie Smith at the wheel.

Below, "Jay Cochran's Snap-on Jaguar looks like it's on the way to a party."

Nebraska and Ohio to Alabama. The organization has 2,500 members and has really taken off since absorbing the Professional Drag Racing Association in 1984. Snap-on became the sponsor of this national series in 1995, is the organization's official tool, and provides top runners with tool packages. There are a number of hot classes in IHRA, perhaps the most exciting Pro Stock. These recognizable automobiles are turning in quarter-mile times below seven seconds. Top Fuel pros sometimes run below five seconds, with terminal speeds approaching 300 miles per hour. A few years earlier, engineers had predicted that no quarter-mile vehicle could exceed 200 miles per hour or so in the quarter. They forgot to tell the mechanics of the IHRA.

There have been many other great Snap-on associations, particularly in the last couple of years. Snap-on has been the official tool of the World of Outlaws dirt-track cars since 1991.

Equally exciting, the company is involved in pickup-truck stadium racing in the persons of Roger Mears and Roger, Jr., and Snap-on helped sponsor Rod Hall in his Hummer during the annual off-road Baja California race. Several top National Hot Rod Association drivers, including Chuck Etchells, the first Nitro Funny Car driver to break the five-second quarter, use Snap-on exclusively. So does TRW/U.S.A., a team of 220 mile per hour Jaguars seen at the 24 Hours of LeMans in France and at courses such as Road America and Sebring.

A turbocharged four-cylinder Ford backfires through its exhaust. Ford has flirted with many forms of racing; its successes include winning the 24 Hours of LeMans with the Mark IV coupe. *Courtesy Road America*

Right, NHRA Top Fuel racer Eddie Hill lights up the tires at a drag-racing meet. Snap-on was a sponsor of the Pontiac-powered dragster.

Believed? Trusted? Loved? *Followed everywhere?* Until Tom and Ray Magliozzi began broadcasting their weekly, one-hour show all across the U.S. on National Public Radio, most people would have been hard pressed to name a mechanic besides the one where they took their car to be serviced. "Click and Clack, the Tappet Brothers," have changed all that.

The hosts of "Car Talk," the Magliozzi brothers dispense irreverent car advice in the broad accent of the tough, east-Cambridge, Massachusetts, neighborhood where they grew up. Spurred by the popularity of their program, Tom and Ray also have a widely syndicated newspaper question-and-answer column and have published a book titled *Car Talk,* both of which provide humorous and helpful advice on car maintenance.

Tom and Ray both graduated from the Massachusetts Institute of Technology. Tom, who also holds degrees from Boston University and Northeastern University, previously worked as a marketing executive in the Boston area. Ray was a VISTA volunteer in Texas before becoming a junior high school teacher in Vermont.

In 1973, the brothers decided to open a do-it-yourself garage in Cambridge. Originally called Hacker's Haven, then the Good News Garage, the business was designed to provide rented space and tools to clients fixing their own cars. As hippies turned into yuppies and car repair became more complicated, the Magliozzi brothers began to offer more conventional car-repair service.

In 1976, Tom was invited to the studios of National Public Radio member station WBUR-FM in Boston, along with other area mechanics, to discuss car repair on a talk show. Tom accepted the invitation and when he was invited back the following week, he brought his brother along. The two subsequently were given their own weekly program, "Car Talk," which soon attracted a large local following. In 1987, National Public Radio began distributing the program coast to coast.

Tom Magliozzi left the Good News Garage in 1978 to

Tom (left) and Ray Magliozzi are well-educated, articulate mechanics whose expertise and sense of humor can be heard on a popular, nationally broadcast weekly show, "Car Talk," from National Public Radio.

teach at Boston University while studying for a doctorate in marketing. Currently, he is teaching at Suffolk University in Boston. Ray, who over the years taught adult education automotive courses and worked on auto-industry complaints as a consultant to the Consumer Affairs Division of the Massachusetts attorney general's office, still runs the shop.

It's tough to keep a good mechanic away from his work.

Anticipating the New Models

Racing provides answers, but here's a nonracing question that's commonly asked the corporation . . . How is Snap-on able to anticipate tool needs—weeks, even months before a new car model is unveiled? Dick Nelsen, a staff engineer, is one of numerous Snap-on people with lousiness in Detroit. "We see new cars years ahead of time," he says. "We're in constant communication with OEMs to find out what's going to change. These aren't just 'contacts,' they're our friends. They may have titles like 'advance service-ability engineer,' but part of their job is to work with us."

An eighteen-year employee, Nelsen notes that working on cars has become more difficult as additional technology is crammed into a compartment that keeps decreasing in size. He points out

Below, a Roger Penske IndyCar pit crew—and its Snap-on tools—awaits its car and driver. Penske cars have won the Indy 500 ten times.

that every vehicle from a popular sports car to a well-received van has spark plugs that require a wheel to be removed or part of the steering system to be dismantled before all plugs can be completely changed. Clearly, tool needs change. In addition to devising tools for Detroit, Snap-on works closely with foreign manufacturers, many of whom have offices on the West Coast. Nelsen and others also are in contact with the truck and diesel industry and with aerospace, though in the latter case the tool volume is much smaller.

"There is one other way we stay in touch," he says, reaching for a short stack of sheets provided by various dealers. These are requests for new and different tools from the field—provided by mechanics who know exactly what is required for them to maintain their productivity. Nelsen and his peers bring back information for everyone, not just tool designers, so that the company is uniformly state of the art. At the moment, the 1998 California Air Resources Board's decision that 2 percent of all cars produced by a manufacturer must be nonpolluting has his attention. Carmakers are working with batteries and with either compressed or liquid natural gas to meet the requirement. When such a car is introduced, Snap-on will have tools in the back shop awaiting it.

Anticipating needs was a priority of Marion F. Gregory's. He served the company as its president from 1985 to 1991. During that same period a sixty-five mile-per-hour speed limit was enacted on rural interstate highways and Chrysler bought American Motors (1987), the importer of Yugos sought bankruptcy protection (1989), and the first new General Motors division since 1918 produced an exciting compact car called the Saturn (1990). The time between when a car was conceived and when it rolled off the assembly line shrunk dramatically as automakers realized how important it was to be first with an original automotive approach. In an information-heavy age, there was a great deal of interesting auto info . . .

The U.S. Department of Commerce looked at 1990 Bureau of the Census figures and came up with a batch of fascinating numbers of interest to people with cars. For example, an overwhelming 86.5 percent of us drive or ride in cars, vans, or trucks to work. In America's largest cities, only one—New York City—has more riders of public transportation than occupants of private vehicles. San Jose has an overwhelming 91.5 percent of its workforce riding privately while a very different metropolis, Indianapolis, is second at 91.4. If you thought public transport was least popular in Los Angeles, think again. Some 10.5 percent of all Angelenos ride to work in public conveyances, compared to a mere 2.7 percent in Jacksonville, and 3.3 percent in both Indianapolis and Phoe-nix.

The economic importance of automobiles involves more than just producing cars. There are more than 500,000 auto-related businesses employing about twelve million workers—10 percent of the American workforce. The industry's huge consumption of raw materials also means jobs, as a typical full-size car consists of 1,500 pounds of steel, 500 pounds of iron, 200 pounds of plastic and 100 pounds each of aluminum and rubber. An interesting statistic shows the auto industry's reach: A large steel mill, hundreds of miles from Detroit but dependent on carmakers to buy its products, uses more water each production day than does all of New York City.

Building cars has gone global. Some two dozen countries are assembling passenger vehicles at the moment, from Australia to Malaysia to states in the former communist country of Yugoslavia. Toyota passed General Motors as the largest manufacturer of cars in 1990 and now has plants in Australia, South Africa, and the U.S., as well as in Japan. Nine manufacturers—Chrysler, Ford, General Motors, Honda, Mazda, Mitsubishis, Nissan, Subaru, and Toyota—currently produce cars in the U.S., and BMW and Mercedes-Benz plan to assemble cars here soon. It's getting tougher to tell who is making what, since Mitsubishi and Chrysler, Mazda and Ford, Nissan and Ford, and Toyota and General Motors all have created vehicles cooperatively.

The big winner, of course, is the consumer. Consider these recent innovations:

Inside a contemporary Snap-on van, a dealer carries virtually any tool a mechanic or a technician might require. Dealers are limited only by their imaginations—Snap-on use is now common on flight lines, in municipal facilities, on large agricultural operations, and in well-equipped home garages.

• CFC-free air conditioning that has made air standard equipment on many vehicles.
• Engines that routinely last more than 100,000 miles with nothing more than regular maintenance.

A 1995 Mercury Mystique, one version of the compact world car that is expected to be a big seller for Ford into the next century. The vehicle comes with a choice of two different four-cylinder engines. *Courtesy Ford Motor Company*

• Tires that adhere as well to wet pavement as last year's tires stuck in dry weather.

• Power steering characteristics that change with the car's speed and direction.

• Crumple zones, side-impact bars, hood-release designs, and other phenomena that make an accident a less dangerous prospect than it was in the past.

• Systems that deliver filtered outside air, unparalleled sound, and a barrage of information on how the car is working as it runs.

• Engine-transmission combinations that provide rapid acceleration, silent cruising, and superior gas mileage.

• Turbochargers and superchargers offer yesterday's power and today's efficiency, awaiting the operator to step down on the accelerator.

• New models come out quicker and work better. Wild ideas like Chrysler's Prowler hot rod are edging toward showroom floors.

• Speaking of showrooms, a shopper can now visit a Saturn dealerhsip via the Internet.

What will the future bring? Primarily, it will involve new materials, from plastic and porcelain engine parts to exhaust devices that will last the life of the car while scavenging a higher percentage of pollutants before they exit the system. Much of it all will continue to need fasteners and tools to work with them.

The Value of a Good Mechanic

Today's public often takes automobile technology—and the people who work on it— for granted. That was the primary reason why Snap-on launched a $2 million print advertising tribute to automotive technicians in the summer of 1994. "When did you first learn the value of a good mechanic?", the headline asks in each of the first three two-page, full-color ads. They show a boy with a broken wagon, a father attempting to assemble a Christmas bike, and a boy and girl struggling over a soapbox-type racer. There's no other copy except for the Snap-on Tools logo and the following tagline: "A tribute to the automotive technicians who keep us moving."

Simplicity itself, the ad series began in *Sports Illustrated* and was seen in *Time, USA Today, Car Craft, Motor Trend,* and other auto-oriented publications. The campaign, tied to Snap-on's seventy-fifth anniverary, has several goals. Robert A. Cornog, chairman, president, and chief executive officer since 1991, told

Snap-on dealers that the ads, which can be seen adorning Snap-on trucks as rolling billboards, are designed to improve the public's understanding of what the modern auto technician does. The ads also are a salute to the company's core customers. Snap-on offered reproduction posters of the ads for the mechanic's shop. And in an attempt to bring consumer automotive writers up to speed, the company held a two-day national conference in 1994 in Chicago, dealing with the computerization of cars.

As absolutely vital as mechanics have always been to Snap-on, these faithful customers may not know that the corporation actually has four divisions. The one they see is, of course, Snap-on Tools, staffed by the dealers who pay them regular visits. But there is also Snap-on Diagnostics, offering computer-controlled automotive diagnostic systems as well as electronic and shop equipment through Snap-on/Sun Tech Systems.

There is Snap-on Industrial, responsible for the products sold in volume to manufacturing and government. And there is Snap-on Financial Services, which covers everything from lease and credit financing to customers to start-up financing of Snap-on franchises.

If the future is as good as the immediate past, both Snap-on and the auto industry are in for an upthrust ride toward the new century. In 1994, new-car sales exceeded fifteen million units, up from the previous record, 14.2 million, in 1993. Here are some other interesting facts:

- For the first time since 1990, the United States produced more cars than Japan.
- Domestic automakers made a lot of money. Chrysler profits were up 20 percent, Ford up 25 percent, General Motors up 14.5, all from 1993.

Here are a pair of Ford idea cars from 1991: Zig is in the foreground, Zag is toward the rear. Detroit has greatly shortened the time it takes for a car to move from the drawing board to the assembly line.

- The average new-car transaction reached $20,000, with one in four cars being leased.
- Pickups, minivans, and sport-utility vehicles accounted for 40 percent of the market.
- U.S. plants assembling Japanese cars became increasingly important to the Japanese because of the continued strength of the yen.
- Car and truck exports to Mexico climbed in the wake of the North American Free Trade Agreement (NAFTA).

before it reported $4 billion in 1994 sales by seeking to increase his stake to 15 percent. Ford started a global reorganization and announced a stock split while G.M. introduced a number of new models and saw an end to the federal government's investigation of its 1973-78 full-size pickups with the fuel tanks mounted outside the frame rails.

The Great New '95s

As good as most news was, it wasn't any more well received then the very latest vehicles from domestic and foreign manufacturers. Ford wouldn't restyle the Taurus, America's best-selling car, until 1996. That means the Honda Accord, redone for 1994, could take the sales title away—unless edged by Ford's sensational new compacts, the Ford Contour and the Mercury Mystique. G.M. introduced a new four-door sport-utility vehicle, to be known in Chevrolet lingo as the Tahoe and in GMC parlance as the Yukon, plus an improved Chevy Cavalier and a new Pontiac, the Sunfire. Chrysler excited prospects with the Cirrus, 1995's *Motor Trend* Car of the Year and a vehicle which also has incarnations as a Dodge and a Plymouth. Toyota Camrys, assembled in Kentucky, continue to be judged the country's best put-together vehicle, while Nissan in Tennessee has a whole new generation of sedans and sporty cars.

Despite the incredible progress, work remains to be done. Each year, worldwide, motor vehicle accidents kill an estimated

In related news, Chrysler's largest shareholder, billionaire Kirk Kerkorian, showed confidence in the company even before it reported $4 billion in 1994 sales by seeking to increase his

300,000 persons. As many as 50,000 of those are Americans, many of whom are young. In fact, more Americans between the ages of five and thirty-two died as a result of traffic accidents than from any other cause. Young people also have higher accident rates than others. Because cars are much safer and roads are in reasonable repair, two-thirds of all accidents are the direct result of driver error. Some 40 percent of all fatalities are attributed to alcohol, which slows reflexes, reduces concentration, and impairs vision. Until the encouraging campaign against drinking and driving succeeds, deaths will continue.

Less frightening but of concern is the continuing ability for the average American to afford a new car. Per capita income is eroding in this country, with car-making competitors such as Canada, Germany, Japan, and Sweden better educating tomorrow's workers and consumers. Despite the affluence of others, however, the United States continues to be the place where goods and services meet and are traded. Such pacts as the General Agreement on Trades and Tariffs (GATT) are expected to help America's balance of payments, where at the moment imports far outweigh exports. This lack of balance is of particular concern between the governments of the U.S. and Japan. The Japanese are exporters who view a free-market economy with skepticism.

What will the next quarter-century hold for automobiles and for Snap-on, now a $1.2 billion-a-year corporation? There are no guarantees, but the public reception of today's cars indicates that the love affair America began with automobiles more than 100 years ago is in no danger of ending. So long as the romance continues, Snap-on's people, products, and services will be making regular calls.

INDEX